D1460357

In Search of
Thérèse

THE WAY OF THE CHRISTIAN MYSTICS

GENERAL EDITOR
Noel Dermot O'Donoghue, ODC

Volume 3

In Search of Thérèse

by

Patricia O'Connor

A Michael Glazier Book
THE LITURGICAL PRESS
Collegeville, Minnesota

About the Author

Patricia O'Connor received her Ph.D. in history from Union Graduate School, Yellow Springs, Ohio. She is a freelance writer of numerous book reviews and articles. Her most recent published book is *Thérèse of Lisieux: A Biography.*

Acknowledgements

Permission has been granted by the Institute of Carmelite Studies to reprint excerpts from the following sources:

Story of a Soul translated by John Clarke, O.C.D. Copyright © 1975, 1976 by Washington Province of Discalced Carmelites ICS Publications 2131 Lincoln Road, N.E. Washington, D.C.

St. Thérèse of Lisieux: Her Last Conversations translated by John Clarke, O.C.D. Copyright © 1977 by Washington Province of Discalced Carmelites ICS Publications 2131 Lincoln Road, N.E. Washington, D.C. 20002

St. Thérèse of Lisieux General Correspondence I translated by John Clarke, O.C.D. Copyright © 1982 by Washington Province of Discalced Carmelites ICS Publications 2131 Lincoln Road, N.E. Washington, D.C. 20002

The Collected Works of St. John of the Cross, trans. by Kieran Kavanaugh, O.C.D., and Otilio Roderiguez, O.C.D. Copyright © 1979 by Washington Province of Discalced Carmelites ICS Publications 2131 Lincoln Road, N.E. Washington, D.C. 20002.

Permission has also been granted by Our Sunday Visitor, Inc. to reprint excerpts from *St. Thérèse of Lisieux by those who knew her.* Ed. and trans. by Christopher O'Mahoney, O.C.D. Copyright © 1979.

Typography by S. Almeida.
Cover design by Placid Stuckenschneider, O.S.B.

2   3   4   5   6   7   8   9

Library of Congress Cataloging-in-Publication Data

O'Connor, Patricia (Patricia M.)
    In search of Thérèse / by Patricia O'Connor.
    p.   cm. — (The Way of the Christian mystics ; v. 3)
    "A Michael Glazier book."
    Includes bibliographical references and index.
    ISBN 0-8146-5596-3
    1. Thérèse, de Lisieux, Saint. 1873–1897. 2. Christian saints-
-France—Lisieux—Biography. 3. Mysticism—Catholic Church-
-History—19th century. 4. Catholic Church—Doctrines-
-History—19th century. 5. Mysticism—France—History—19th
century.   I. Title.   II. Series.
BX4700.T5025   1990
282'.092'4—dc19
[B]   86-45343
                                              CIP

For
Linda McMahon

Table of Contents

Editor's Preface

Up to quite recently mystics were either misunderstood or simply not understood. But now we are coming to see that, in T.S. Eliot's words, the way of the mystics is "our only hope, or else despair." As the darkness deepens, and the lights go out, those ancient lights begin to appear and to show us the way forward. They are not only lights to guide us, but are each a human countenance in which we can recognise something of ourselves—each is a portrait for self-recognition.

Unfortunately, the great Christian mystics have been generally presented as models of perfection or monuments of orthodoxy—sometimes, too, as inhumanly joyless and ascetical. Yet they were, above all else, men and women of feeling, always vulnerable, at times perhaps insecure and uncertain of the way ahead. For all that, they all shine with a special divine likeness and a special human radiance.

Each of the following portraits tries to present a true likeness of its subject, a likeness that comes alive especially in the ordinary and the everyday. In each case the author has been asked to enliven scholarship with personal warmth, and to temper enthusiasm with accurate scholarship. Each portrait hopes to be in its own way a work of art, something carefully and lovingly fashioned out of genuine material.

The main focus nevertheless is on the way in which each mystic mediates the Christian Gospel, and so gives us a deeper, richer, clearer vision of the Christian mystery. This kind of exposition demands the reader's full and prayerful attention. Each book is the story of a pilgrimage, for the mystic, the writer and the reader.

Noel O'Donoghue

Acknowledgements

I am deeply grateful to members of the community of the Carmel of Lisieux for their unfailing cooperation both in providing sources and verifying details. I am also indebted to Father James Peterson for his insights into contemplative prayer, Jean Laport and Ellen Weaver of the University of Notre Dame, and the staff of the Wittenberg University Library for locating 19th century French sources, and Leanne Wierenga and Barbara Kaiser for advice on translation.

That this study was possible at all is due in large part to the careful translations into English of primary sources by Father John Clarke, O.C.D., and to the Institute for Carmelite Studies which permitted me to quote extensively from their publications.

Finally, I am grateful to my husband, Joseph O'Connor, for reading and criticizing the complete manuscript.

Chronology

1873	January 2: Born in Alençon, France.
	March: Sent to live on a farm with Rose Taillé.
1874	April 2: Returns to her mother permanently.
1877	August 28: Her mother dies of breast cancer.
	November 15: The Martins move to Lisieux to live near their relatives, the Guérins.
1881	October 3: Thérèse, age 8 1/2, begins school at the Benedictine Abbey, Lisieux.
1882	October 2: Thérèse loses her "second mother" Pauline to the cloister. By the end of the year she has "a constant headache."
1883	March 25: Start of six weeks of a nervous illness and hallucinations.
1886	Recurrent headaches. Age 13 Thérèse leaves school for good.
	October 15: Marie Martin, the third person to raise Thérèse, leaves home to join the Carmel.
	Christmas: Thérèse's "conversion": an abrupt change in her personality after the Midnight Mass.
1887	May 29: Asks her father's permission to enter the Carmel.
	November: trip to Rome. Opposed by the Carmel's clerical superior, Thérèse asks Pope Leo XIII's permission to enter the Carmel.

1888	April 9: Enters the Carmel of Lisieux.
1889	January 10: Receives the Habit.
	February 12: Her father is committed to Bon Sauveur, a mental hospital.
1890	September 8: Profession.
	September 24: Receives the Carmelite Veil.
1893	February 2: Writes her first poem.
1894	July 29: Her father dies. In September Céline joins her in the Carmel of Lisieux, raising to four the number of Martin sisters within it.
	December: Ordered to write her childhood memories (Manuscript A of *Story of a Soul*).
1895	June 11: Offers herself formally as a "Victim of Holocaust to God's Merciful Love."
1896	January 20: Delivers her copybook of memories to Pauline.
	Good Friday: first coughs up blood. Within a few days enters into the "thickest darkness."
	September: Letter to Marie: "My Vocation is Love" (Manuscript B of *Story of a Soul*).
1897	June: writes of her spiritual insights for her obituary letter to other Carmels (Manuscript C of *Story of a Soul*).
	September 30 dies of tuberculosis. Age 24.

Thérèse's Family

Parents:

Zélie Martin - Revealed most clearly through her blunt, lively letters filled with stories and details of daily life. After giving birth to eight children in less than eleven years and seeing four of them die she wanted one more child, determined that it should live. This was Thérèse, whose life Zélie saved by walking all night to a wetnurse in the country. As strong a businesswoman as she was a mother, she ran a lacemaking business from her home. Died of breast cancer.

Louis Martin - A reserved, gentle man with no pretensions, who would have been a priest had he known Latin. In time abandoned his own watchmaking trade to manage his wife's lace business. The Church, his wife, his daughters were his life. Practiced a quiet, prayerful religious life: attended daily Mass, took pilgrimages, donated large sums of money to the Church. Age 54 when his wife died, his affection grew deeper for 4 year old Thérèse whom he called his "little queen." Always kind and warm toward her, he could not grasp her inner struggles. At the close of his life he spent three years in a mental hospital.

Sisters:

Marie - the oldest of the 5 Martin girls, 13 years older than Thérèse. Mother to Thérèse for 4 years, Marie dealt well and strictly with her youngest sister's self-torment at age 12 and 13. Thérèse depended on her oldest sister without ever truly warming to her. At times Thérèse balked against Marie's "cantankerous" personality (GCI, p.153). Considered Thérèse, even at age 14, "always a baby." Entered the Carmel of Lisieux with belief in God's call but no emotion.

Pauline - 11 years older than Thérèse, and Thérèse's childhood idol. Served as a second Mother to Thérèse after Zélie Martin's death, though Pauline was just under 16 years of age herself. Triggered an emotional illness in Thérèse when she left home to enter the Carmelite monastery in Lisieux when Thérèse was 9 1/2: "*my Pauline* behind the *grille.*" Later served as Thérèse's Prioress for three years and sat by her bedside for four months as she was dying, recording all their conversations.

Léonie - 9 years older than Thérèse, "poor Léonie," whom their mother worried over from infancy. A troubled child and the sister most distant from Thérèse. Failing an attempt in the convent just before Thérèse was to enter the Carmelites, Léonie tried to dissuade Thérèse from the hard convent life. After yet another failed attempt, she finally entered once more after Thérèse's death, and remained.

Céline - 4 years older than Thérèse and Thérèse's closest companion as she grew. Their correspondence after Thérèse entered Carmel revealed Thérèse's struggles and insights while their father was in a mental hospital. Entered the same cloister after Louis Martin's death, bringing with her a camera with which she took photographs of Thérèse (rare within cloistered walls) which reveal both her deepening inner life and the illness that killed her. Brought with her also some hand-copied books of the Old Testament which she gave to Thérèse, providing Thérèse her only copy of the Bible. In these pages Thérèse found a biblical basis for the insights she already had. An artist, Céline painted pictures of her sister which, over the years, became more and more saccharine, the best known showing a haloed Thérèse cradling roses. Céline's pictures were distributed by the millions in place of the fine and revealing photographs which she herself had taken.

Other Relatives:

Céline Guérin - Thérèse's aunt. A Fournet, one of the wealthy and socially prominent families of Lisieux. Warm and indulgent, Céline Guérin welcomed Thérèse kindly into their home and on seaside vacations, but had no grasp of Thérèse's inner life.

Isidore Guérin - Zélie Martin's brother and guardian of the five girls after her death. An external man, he treated Thérèse kindly but frightened her with his loud singing and voice. Believed the family overindulged her, and set in motion the 10 year old Thérèse's hysterical illness by reminiscing about her dead mother. Isidore Guérin initially opposed Thérèse's entry to the Carmel; made the decision to place her father in a mental institution; helped publish *Story of a Soul*; wrote for a Catholic paper from an anti-semitic and pro-clergy bias. After his niece's death, baffled by the public's reaction to Thérèse's *Story of a Soul,* the pilgrims that poured into Lisieux to visit her grave, and the suggestion that she was a saint, he initially opposed her canonization but withdrew his objections.

Marie Guérin - 3 years older than Thérèse and a common childhood companion. Tormented by a sense of sin at age 18 she turned to her younger cousin in the convent for help. Joined the Carmelites, became a novice under Thérèse, and chronicled Thérèse's cheerfulness during her final illness in a series of letters home to her family.

Jeanne Guérin - 5 years older than Thérèse and the only one of the 7 Martin-Guérin cousins to marry. Her husband, Francis La Néele, tended Thérèse during her final illness when the Carmel doctor was on vacation. It was he who diagnosed tuberculosis.

I

Beneath the Legend

"As long as I knew her, the only part of her that
touched the ground were the soles of her feet."[1]
Pauline Martin
Testimony from the Process of Beatification

"I am the *very small brush* he deigns to use...for the
smallest details."[2]
Thérèse—1897 (Age 24)

To glimpse the inner life of St. Thérèse we must first get
past the language of sanctity. This language is encased in
vague phrases hinting at the otherworldly, phrases which
blunt those human details through which we know a person.
Since Thérèse Martin died in 1897 leaving behind many
letters, notes, photographs, written memories and people
who lived with her, we might expect her to be an exception.
The first Church tribunal convened in 1910, a mere 13 years
after her death, recording many first hand memories of her a
relatively short time after the events themselves, an investiga-

[1]TE, p. 41.
[2]C, p. 235.
*A guide to references and abbreviations appears on p. 192.

tion unique in the modern Church. The tribunal did elicit personal recollections; but the wording of the questions suggested a certain framework in which to view a saint. Witnesses were asked, for example, to comment on the "heroism of her virtues generally":

> . . .the witness shall be asked whether to his knowledge the Servant of God displayed uncommon fervor, constancy, and eagerness throughout her life for the practice of virtue generally. If this answer is affirmative, he shall illustrate by what deeds of hers can this excellence or "heroism" be probed, suitably circumstantiating his examples. . .[3]

There were many other questions as well, but the words all evoked the heroic tradition of sanctity. Memories obliged. By this time everyone who knew Thérèse had memories of her shining with piety; most recalled noticing the seeds of sanctity. A few months before the tribunal convened Victoire Pasquier, the Martin family maid, told Pauline Martin, ". . .I was very fond of you all, but Thérèse had something that none of you had. There was something angelic about her. . ."[4]

Perhaps. But in *Story of a Soul* Thérèse herself testifies to another opinion of her held by Victoire, one the maid apparently forgot amidst the general talk of haloed recollections. Thérèse's story:

> I wanted an inkstand which was on the shelf of the fireplace in the kitchen; being too little to take it down, I very nicely asked Victoire to give it to me, but she refused telling me to get up on a chair. I took a chair without saying a word but thinking she wasn't too nice; wanting to make her feel it, I searched out in my little head what offended me the most. She often called me "a little brat"

[3]TE, p. 14.
[4]TE, p. 65.

when she was annoyed at me ...So *before jumping off*
my chair, I turned around with *dignity* and said: "Victoire, you are a brat!" Then I made my escape, leaving her
to meditate on the profound statement I had just made.
...soon I heard her shouting: 'M'amz'ell Marie. Thérèse
just called me a brat!' Marie came and made me ask
pardon, and I did so without having contrition. I thought
that if Victoire didn't want to stretch her *big arm* to do me
a *little service*, she merited the title *brat*.[5]

In Thérèse's description both personalities spring to life. Her
speech bristles with simple, concrete language and details,
not the abstract language of "heroism." This distinction is
significant.

Despite stories of her "angelic" eyes, look, face and hair,
despite some family members sentimentally calling her "a
little saint", while Thérèse lived only one person came close
to recognizing her true sanctity and that was shortly before
she died. Those around her were wedded to the heroic
notion of "The Saint" and Thérèse Martin did not fit this
mold. But it is not true that she was more the "brat" than the
"angel"; the current trend to humanize religious figures by
reducing them to such a *cliché* would distort Thérèse as
badly as the haloed pictures. To grasp her way of sanctity we
must abandon such categories to examine her real life, for
Thérèse Martin cut a path to God for ordinary people.

* * * * *

The person who came closest to glimpsing a little of the
true power of Thérèse's insights and inner life while she lived
was her sister Pauline, and the story of how she noticed her
sister's uniqueness is revealing.

One winter night after evening prayer four of the Martin
sisters clustered about the single fire in the Lisieux Carmel.
Thérèse was telling stories of her childhood, and a good

[5]A, p. 39.

story teller she was—a mimic, with a sharp recall of the incidents.

"What a pity we haven't got all that in writing!" Marie said.

"I couldn't ask for anything better," said Pauline, the Carmel Prioress, and ordered Thérèse to write down her memories.[6] Thérèse was very exact about orders. For the next year she spent any hour free from her regular duties writing her memories. The following January she slipped her copybook to Pauline as she passed her stall in the choir. Pauline nodded and casually put the little copybook aside until she found time to read it—two months later.[7]

What Pauline read astonished her. Though Thérèse was 23 and they had shared monastic life for 8 years (during three of which Pauline served as her Prioress), Pauline felt she was seeing her youngest sister clearly for the first time.

"...how I regretted not having thanked her sooner, for she so deserved this! My little Thérèse!...I said to myself: And this blessed child...is still in our midst! I can speak to her, see her, touch her. Oh! How unknown she is here! And how I am going to appreciate her more now!"[8]

A year later Pauline experienced a second shock of insight. During that time she had watched a persistent cough and sore throat gradually weaken Thérèse until finally she gave up her monastic duties. Thérèse was fading; the mysterious illness baffled Pauline. On the last Saturday in May, 1897, Thérèse's back was punctured repeatedly with red-hot cauterizing needles.[9] Still not considered sick enough to be in the infirmary, she went back to her cell to lie down on her straw mattress laid on a wood frame.[10] The next day Thérèse finally cleared up the mystery of her illness and shocked her sister. She told Pauline that she began to cough up blood

[6]TE, p. 33.
[7]*Ibid.*
[8]LA, p. 18, (Quoted from DE, p. 35).
[9]DE, p. 152.
[10]ME, p. 214.

more than a year earlier.[11] During much of that time Thérèse continued to rise before 6:00 am, to observe all the hours of prayer, to work in the laundry room, and even to fast. Sitting in Thérèse's cell on that Sunday in May, 1897 Pauline realized that Thérèse was dying. Throughout the last summer as she tended her sister through the gruesome final stages of tuberculosis Pauline was frightened; Thérèse was not.

"I have known a good many really fervent Carmelites," Pauline testified 13 years later, "nuns who loved God and feared to offend him, but Sister Thérèse's state of soul was so different from what I have seen in others that they seem to have nothing in common. Such was the intimacy of her union with God that you would have thought she was always able to see him."[12]

"How unknown she is here." Pauline—the person we might expect to know Thérèse most intimately—only recognized this "state of soul" toward the end of Thérèse's life as she read her childhood memories and nursed her to her death. It is not the purpose of this book to explain St. Thérèse according to the fixed categories of sanctity lodged in Pauline Martin's mind and the minds of the other nuns in the Carmel who did not "recognize" Thérèse. Nor is it the purpose to chip away at her popular image merely to bring her down to human size. The objective is rather to glimpse that distinctive state of soul with which others seemed "to have nothing in common" by examining some of the rough, unpolished details of her days, and her understanding of God as it took shape while she lived.

* * * * *

Like any child, Thérèse received her ideas of God from the ordinary people about her. All were Catholic, but each had a distinct personality and reflected different elements of a vast and varied tradition. These people ranged from her gentle,

[11]LA, p. 53.
[12]TE, p. 46.

quiet Father, Louis Martin, who recited poetry to her as she sat on his lap[13] and who liked to make pilgrimages, to her bombastic Uncle Isidore, a "militant Christian" connected with a monarchist newspaper during the Dreyfus Era (1890's).[14] Her task was to carve out her *own* way from what she saw, heard and was taught.

Thérèse's earliest religious training came from her mother, Zélie, a realistic businesswoman whose sense of humor shines through this passage from a letter she wrote when Thérèse was a child:

"Baby is a little imp; she'll kiss me and at the same time wish me to die. 'Oh, how I wish you would die, dear little Mother!' When I scold her she answers: 'it is because I want you to go to heaven, and you say we must die to get there!' She wishes the same for her Father in her outbursts of affection for him."[15]

Thérèse liked that passage; she quoted it in her own written memories. Zélie had a lasting impact on her, but she died when Thérèse was 4½.

After that Thérèse heard about God primarily from 16 year old Pauline. But Thérèse's "second mother" Pauline left home to join the cloistered Carmel of Lisieux 5 years later. For Thérèse the shock was worse than her mother's death. Direct contact was severed except for group visits of one half hour a week at the end of which Thérèse had a couple of minutes alone with Pauline, which she spent in tears. The shock triggered a six week illness with hallucinations. From this segment of a letter written at the end of that illness we can form some idea of Pauline's sentimental approach to religion and to life, in contrast to her mother's lively realism. Pauline writes the 9½ year old Thérèse:

> ...Look, how blue the sky is! From time to time I see little swallows passing by, gay and light, just like a little

---

[13]A, p. 43.
[14]DE, pp. 859, 60.
[15]A, p. 17.

girl in good health...and I pray to the dwellers of this very blue heaven to have a little pair of wings fall down from on high for my own swallow. With this pair of wings she would run through the fields, she would play in the beautiful sun, she would come and rest from time to time in her Agnes'[16] very sweet nest, up there high on the mount of Carmel where the weather is so good, so good! and where one breathes in heaven's air and is always able to see, even during the winter, the sun and flowers...[17]

At school Thérèse heard another voice of the tradition, sharply different from both Zélie's and Pauline's, in the person of the chaplain, the Abbé Domin. According to Thérèse's notes from a retreat made when she was 12:

"What the abbé told us was frightening. He spoke about mortal sin, and he described a soul in the state of sin and how much God hated it. He compared it to a little dove soaked in mud, and who is no longer able to fly."[18]

After this retreat Thérèse's world became a torment in which any stray thought might cause God to hate her soul. She left the Abbey School. Home all day at age 13 she withdrew for hours at a time into an attic that resembled a chapel dedicated to Pauline. It was the room that Pauline had used for painting before she left home.

"It was a real bazaar," Thérèse writes in her memories,

an assemblage of pious objects and curiosities, a garden, and an aviary. Thus, at the far end on the wall was a *big cross* in black wood, without a corpus, and several drawings I liked. On another wall, a basket, decorated with muslin and pink ribbons, contained some delicate herbs

[16]Pauline's name in religious life was Sister Agnes of Jesus.

[17]Pauline to Thérèse, LC 13, May 14, 15 (?) 1883, GC I, p. 172.

[18]Jean-Francois Six, *La Veritable Enfance de Thérèse de Lisieux, Nervrose et Saintete,* (Paris, Editions du Seuil, 1972), p. 201. (Thérèse's retreat notes quoted from P. Francois de Sainte-Marie: Notes et Tables, pp. 22-27.)

and flowers. Finally, on the last wall, was enthroned all by itself the portrait of *Pauline* at the age of ten.[19]

But this isolated world which Thérèse so carefully sculpted, piece by piece, failed her. Within months she was jarred by the news that her oldest sister Marie would desert her to join Pauline at the Carmel. Marie, "the only support which attached me to life!" Marie's news spoiled Thérèse's attic retreat: "my *room* lost its attraction for me. . ."[20] The 13 year old child who wept because she forgot the flowers for her mother's grave, who became ill at the seashore with her cousins because she was away from home for a couple of days, left the security of her attic room to come downstairs to a nearly empty house. For the third time in her young life the person she trusted as a mother abandoned her.

At this point in her life a critical change occurred: she no longer looked to those about her to explain what she must do. Two months after Marie left home, on Christmas Eve, Thérèse began the final period of her life. She called the experience a "conversion." That night she saw her life clearly, dropped all excuses for her behavior, and began, she said, *"to run as a giant!"* In an apparent paradox which hints at a resolution to come, she said too, that she regained the "strength of soul which she had lost at the age of 4½."[21]

Ready to begin to examine her tradition for herself, Thérèse began a practice that would transform her way of understanding the truth of the religion in which she and all her family believed. She took to reading on her own. From the pages of *The Imitation of Christ* a distinctive voice spoke to her. In personal and powerful terms Thomas à Kempis spoke of self-discipline and of the love of Jesus. At age 14 Thérèse sat down "by the window of my study" to read words that formed a perfect counterpoint to the self-centered

[19]A, p. 90.
[20]A, p. 91.
[21]A, pp. 97 & 98.

years since the age of 8½, those she called "the saddest years."

The first step was self-control; even at age 13 Thérèse cried continuously. Until her Christmas "conversion" she had viewed each outburst singly, explained by something outside happening *to* her: she cried *because* she forgot the flowers for her mother's grave; she was sad, weepy, withdrawn *because* her sister Marie left home. In a critical decision, Thérèse no longer explained her outbursts by any circumstance.

"I desired the grace," she wrote later, quoting Thomas à Kempis, "'of having absolute control over my actions, of not being their slave but their mistress.'"[22] She examined her own behavior in the framework of Thomas' words:

> Because our hearts are frivolous and because we ignore our faults we never discover the sickness in our souls. . .[23]

> If you wish to keep peace and live in harmony with others, you must learn to abdicate your will in many things.[24]

> If we had a spark of true charity within us we would surely perceive the emptiness of all earthly things.[25]

> It is difficult to give up old habits and still more difficult to go against one's own will. But if you do not overcome small and easy things, when will you overcome those that are larger and more troublesome?[26]

At age 14 Thérèse took Thomas à Kempis's path out of the narrow circle of her self. But in Thomas she also read words uncommon in the Martin household. Sin is punished; the damned are punished forever in hell; those not damned but meriting punishment for sin will be purged in purgatory.

[22]A, p. 91.
[23]IC, p. 60.
[24]IC, p. 50.
[25]IC, p. 49.
[26]IC, p. 43.

It is better to purge our sins and root out our vices now, then to keep them for some future purgation. The more lenient you are on yourself and the more you yield to your flesh, the greater will be your future suffering...a man will be punished according to the types of sins he committed. Those who are lazy will be pricked with red-hot spurs, and the glutton will be tormented by acute hunger and thirst. Those filled with lust and who have indulged their senses will howl in pain like mad dogs...[27]

*   *   *   *   *

When Thérèse left school and retreated into Pauline's attic she selected the objects to surround her with such care that years later she recalled them in detail. The list merits a closer look:

"My garden...*suspended* in front of the window"

"...pots of flowers (the rarest I could find);"

"small statues of saints;"

"little baskets made out of shells;"

"a *big cross* in black wood;"

"a ribboned basket with "delicate herbs and flowers;"

"a *large cage*" with "a *great* number of birds;"

"A beautiful *doll's* cot belonging to *Pauline*;"

"the portrait of *Pauline* at the age of ten."[28]

From among all the possible interests of a 13 year old French girl Thérèse chose mainly from three categories: religious objects, things from nature, mementoes of Pauline.

Two years later Thérèse again withdrew from the carefully sculpted life of study, Church, social visits and vacations at

[27]IC, p. 68.
[28]A, pp. 90-91.

the shore with the Guérins. She withdrew into the Lisieux Carmel, another enclosed, restricted space. No less than her home this enclosure contained tangible representations of a particular culture—images, statues, pictures, prayers, music, the arches and stone and cross of the courtyard, the rough thick wool of the habit, the stoneware dishes, the half-hour sand glass. Such things represented the accumulation of hundreds of years of tradition. But although the solitude appealed to her and she was delighted by the simple cell with its beige wool bedspread and boards and straw mattress, this time she was not barricading herself into an isolated secure world, wrapped in beloved mementoes. After the failure of her attic world Thérèse never again tried to shield herself behind a fortress of objects of whatever taste or artistic or religious merit. In place of protective barriers Thérèse culti-vated an *inner* life as selective as her attic world, and there lies her significance: not that she "heroically" lived the pure, ascetic and sacrificial Carmelite life to perfection, or even that she carved out a wholly original path to God, but that she distilled from the tradition of centuries a simple set of insights that echo the core of that tradition in tones which speak to a world skeptical of larger-than-life heroes and grander-than-life deeds.

From the hundreds of pages of pious thoughts, gothic prayers, lives of the saints read aloud in the refectory, from the passages of *Isaiah* and *Tobit* and *Wisdom*, from the psalms chanted during the Divine Office, from the *Rule* and the *Constitutions* of the order, from John of the Cross and Thomas à Kempis, from the advice and personal piety of people as disparate as her sister Pauline and the terrifying Abbé Domin, and most importantly from the words of Jesus, Thérèse selected just those words which contained her own experience of life. These she welded not to the artificial imagery popular in France but to the purest images she saw—images that attracted her from infant days on the farm and attracted her still inside the cloister—the colorful, living images of nature. Despite Thérèse's belief that once the clois-ter door shut behind her she would never again see wildflowers, not only did the cloister not shut out nature, but its starkness accentuated the flowers that were often handed through the turnstile.

* * * * *

Jesus' world, like Thérèse's, was encrusted with customs and attachments: ritual cleanliness, sacred meals, sacrifices of animals at the temple, pilgrimages to the holy mountain where one might worship God at The Temple, rules governing clean and unclean food. At the core of this tradition was imbedded a central mystery barely discernible amidst the swarm of customs. With fresh words, fresh images, fresh insights into the familiar ancient Scriptures Jesus conveyed a new sense of God: not the distant judge awaiting in his remote heaven the sacrifice of animals to his sense of justice, but a Father. This image of God, simple, clear, intimate, loving, provided the priests with their excuse for killing him: blasphemy, a greater threat than healing on the sabbath.

His followers, even his closest friends, failed to grasp what he taught them. Shocked when he was dragged off to die, they scattered. What Jesus' words failed to make clear he embodied—literally lived out in his body. It was intended as a crude death, a man fastened to a crossbeam of wood like an insect on a pin. Yet only this extreme act drove home his message. Only in his dying and then having life again did they understand. To dislodge people from their assumptions the sign of the New Covenant had to be a ritual powerful and simple enough to sweep aside the empty rituals. It could not be a subtle sign. As Flannery O'Connor has said about a world that no longer hears the truth, for the hard of hearing you must shout. The sign had to be clear enough to shout at men and women numbed by the clutter of images and deafened by the blare of competing words. That sign was, of course, the breaking of his body and the spilling of his blood. It is significant that the disciples on the road to Emmaus recognized him only in the breaking of the bread.

On the purely natural plane Thérèse's life is not only baffling, but shocking. She turned away from life in a family

that could afford to educate her and liked travel, to shut herself up in a set of stone buildings without heat, damp buildings located in the ravine of a river. This was at age 15.
At 17 she vowed to stay for life,
At 22 she offered herself as a Holocaust Victim to God's Love,
At 24 she died of tuberculosis.

This occurred not in Medieval Europe, but a short train ride from Paris in the era of the Eiffel tower, the Impressionists and the health spa, to which her wealthy uncle (and guardian) travelled weeks before Thérèse died to seek a cure for his gout. Like Jesus' crucifixion, Thérèse's death shouts at the modern person numbed with competing words and symbols. Her choices violate not only modern assumptions about education and comfort, but the most basic assumptions about health.

Thérèse lived her belief so literally that her actions stunned even her sister Pauline who had served as the convent's prioress. The mental illness of their father was a brutal blow to the Martin sisters and certainly shook Thérèse. How did she fit this into her trust in God? Pauline testified:

"There is a picture on which she listed all the favours God had done her. Among them is 12 February, 1889—the day our father was admitted to the (mental) institution..."[29]

Thérèse saw her father as another Christ, another Victim; and she saw herself as a Victim as well. Her offering of herself to God was, she insisted, an act of trust, an act of love and not a request for suffering: yet two years later Thérèse died a terrible death without the slightest fear or resistance, as if she expected it. When she first coughed up blood Thérèse simply informed her superior and then neither told her sister Pauline nor sought any help beyond what the current Prioress, a woman committed to strict bodily discipline and ascetic practices, decided should be done. It was this realization that startled Pauline into *seeing* her sister so differently

[29]TE, p. 56.

on that Sunday in May, four months before Thérèse died. Pauline Martin dreaded watching her little sister suffer. Even a good Carmelite Sister like Pauline Martin recoils from crucifixion when it is her little sister being crucified.

Like Jesus, Thérèse embodied, literally, what she believed. Despite the power of her stark, simple life, she, like Jesus has been twisted into many pious, vaguely sentimental shapes. She who described even her attic retreat in the most concrete of words and images—"a *big cross* in black wood," "little baskets made out of shells" was herself abstracted to an imagined ideal of sainthood, all the etchings of her personality and the colorful world in which she lived rubbed away in favor of a haloed face with "angelic" eyes, cradling roses.

One cannot view the inner life of another person directly. To catch sight of Thérèse's inner life we must approach it indirectly, as it appears through her choices; not only the dramatic choice of Carmel and of offering herself to God, not only the choice of how to behave each day amidst people who controlled her actions without understanding her, but also the words, stories, images and passages of scripture she chose from among the vast store of ancient culture which linked certain of the old beliefs and traditions with her own experience of life. Like Jesus, Thérèse lived out the mystery in which she believed; and, like him, she translated that mystery into simple, fresh, common images that speak to the heart of her times.

II

Detachment

"God was able in a very short time to extricate me from
the very narrow circle in which I was turning without
knowing how to come out."[1]
Thérèse

"Make room for Christ and deny entrance to everything
else."[2]
Thomas à Kempis

A revealing fragment in Thérèse's story occurred when
Canon Delatroëtte, the clerical superior of the Carmel of
Lisieux, refused her permission to enter the Carmelite monastery at age 15. The elderly Canon seems stiff, rigid, a man
cemented into his position even after the bishop has relented.
Canon Delatroëtte is a marginal figure destined by a single
act of his life to be preserved in cameo: he blocked the path
of St. Thérèse.

By the yardstick of educated thought the Canon's stance
was not unreasonable. At age 13 Thérèse could not with-
stand the normal convent school life as a day student, yet the

[1]A, p. 101.
[2]IC, p. 79.

following year sought to join her two sisters in the strictly cloistered and austere Carmel. Reason supports Canon Delatroëtte.

His suggested alternative was not unreasonable either, at least on the surface.

"He told me there wasn't any danger in staying at home. I could lead a Carmelite life there, and if I didn't take the discipline all was not lost, etc. etc..."[3] "The Discipline" involved self-inflicted flogging on certain days in the Carmel.[4] Though Thérèse's "etc., etc." conveys her disdain for the Canon's suggestion, a home more devoted to the Catholic faith did not exist in Lisieux. Shortly after they visited the Canon, Louis Martin took Thérèse on a pilgrimage to Rome; he regularly attended daily Mass. The previous summer Thérèse and Céline spent hours speaking of God:

"I don't know if I'm mistaken, but it seems to me the outpourings of our souls were similar to those of St. Monica with her son when, at the port of Ostia, they were lost in ecstasy at the sight of the Creator's marvels! It appears we were receiving graces like those granted to the great saints."[5] Yet Thérèse fought to get out of that household.

"Had I been forced to *pass through flames*," she wrote, "I would have done it..."[6] Thérèse's instincts were right. The point was not how warm or religious her family was, but the effect of the atmosphere on her. How was her family shaping Thérèse?

To begin with, typed as the fragile child, the sick child, Thérèse was indulged:

> I myself didn't do any housework whatsoever. After Marie's entrance into Carmel it sometimes happened that I tried to make up the bed to please God, or else, in the evening, when Céline was away I'd bring in her plants ...if Céline was unfortunate enough not to seem happy

[3]A, p. 111.
[4]Interview with Carmel Prioress, July 22, 1983.
[5]A, p. 104.
[6]A, p. 106.

or surprised because of these little services, I became unhappy and proved it by my tears.[7]

A couple of nights spent at her school at age 11 within walking distance of home brought her father and sisters over to visit each night with "all sorts of pastries."[8] To please her father her long blond hair was curled daily. To her father Thérèse was the "Little Queen;" to her sister Marie she was "the baby." Following a visit from the 14 year old Thérèse, Marie wrote home from the Carmel:

"Darling of my heart, my very tall baby! Yet always a baby in my eyes. . . "[9]

Though the view of Thérèse differed in the household of the uncle and aunt who helped to raise her, it was just as fixed. In a letter back to her husband from a vacation when Thérèse was 11, her aunt Céline's cheerfulness and warmth flow into each line:

"We are all very happy here.Thérèse's face is always radiant with joy. She is enjoying herself very much at sketching; she and Marie have undertaken to do the house on the farm. . . I see two future *artists* in my two pupils. . . "[10] But for all her zest and kindness, Céline Guérin understood Thérèse no better than her husband did. Thérèse's perception of their judgment:

"At Uncle's house. . . I was taken for a little dunce, good and sweet, and with right judgment, yes, but incapable and clumsy. . . They often spoke highly of the intelligence of others in my presence, but of mine they never said a word, and so I concluded I didn't have any. . . "[11] The Guérins embraced middle class life: an elegant home, vacations by the shore, concern over health, encouragement of artistic skills in the children. With their daughters Thérèse was

[7]A, p. 97.

[8]A, p. 75.

[9]Marie to Thérèse, LC 49, May 31 (?) 1887, GCI, p. 269.

[10]Madame Guérin to Isidore Guérin, LD, Aug. 7, 1884, GCI, p. 209.

[11]A, p. 82.

bored by some afternoons spent *"dancing quadrilles."*[12] Such were the boundaries of her home life at age 14, for Thérèse had no friends.

She did have a tutor; but Thérèse's own report conveys the limits of this conventional maiden lady. Madame Papineau lived with her elderly mother and a cat in an "antiquely furnished room."

"When I arrived," wrote Thérèse, "I usually found only old Lady Cochain who looked at me *'with her big clear eyes'* and then called out Ma...d'moiselle...Thérèse est la!... Her daughter answered promptly in an *infantile* voice: 'Here I am *Mama.*'" The lessons took place in the same parlor where the mother, Madame Cochain, chatted with visitors: priests, ladies, young girls. Sometimes they whispered flattering things about Thérèse as she tried to study.[13]

Just as some young French men and women fled the villages that formed them to follow an artistic vision, Thérèse determined to shed her household, her pets, her lessons, the summers sketching at the shore, all that made up the tangible life of the fragile little queen. She craved, she repeats over and over in her writing, to be "hidden." Thérèse could not live the inner life of the desert in the French parlor.

* * * * *

At this point we encounter one of those little inconsistent reactions familiar to every human being but often lost in the stories of saints. So determined was Thérèse to enter the Carmel by Christmas of 1887 that she fought all the way to Rome for permission. At Christmas the bishop remained silent. Everyone about her sympathized; the Carmelites sang her a special song and the 15 year old who had stormed Rome to live the ascetic life of the cloister broke down and cried.[14] Who could doubt that she craved the life of sacrifice with all her young heart?

[12] A, p. 54.
[13] A, p. 85.
[14] GCI, p. 389, and A, p. 142.

But that Christmas yielded up to Thérèse a surprising insight into herself.

"Would you believe," she told Céline years later, "that, in spite of the ...bitterness... I experienced a real pleasure on that Christmas night in wearing my pretty blue hat with the white dove. What tricks this human nature of ours can play on us!"[15]

Her delight in that stylish blue hat sharpens the point: for the inner life to grow, Thérèse had to shut herself off from such distractions.

The following April she at last stepped into the Carmel, at last shed the old identity, only to find it waiting for her: assigned to acquaint her with the Carmel's customs was her oldest sister Marie. As the following incident told from Marie's point of view suggests, Thérèse kindly but firmly resisted Marie's effort to reinstate her as the "baby." When this occurred Thérèse had been praying the divine Office for three weeks:

"...thinking that she (Thérèse) did not know how to find the Office alone I wanted to keep her with me..." Marie reports. "Instead of taking advantage of this opportunity, she answered sweetly: 'I thank you, I found them today. I would be happy to stay with you, but it is better that I deprive myself, for we are not at home!'"[16]

The physical break from the patterns of home was only the first step. No more striking symbol of Thérèse the Little Queen existed than her long blond hair, curled daily to please her father. From the time she was a child Thérèse's hair attracted notice. A local notary public used to pass Thérèse and her father while walking through town.

"I just stopped and stared at her," wrote Mr. Rixe, "that little girl with her mass of golden hair."[17]

[15]ME, p. 26.

[16]NPPO 1908, pp. 6-7, quoted in GCI, p. 428, ft. 6.

[17]Quoted in Peter-Thomas Rohrback, O.C.D., *Photo Album of St. Thérèse of Lisieux*, (NY: P.J. Kenedy and Sons, 1962), p. 22.

At the ceremony of clothing in the brown woolen habit and the veil of the Carmelites Thérèse's thick blond curls tumbled down her wedding dress. After clothing in the Habit it was the custom to cut the novices's hair. An exception was made for Thérèse, and she balked.

"'You are too young,' I told her," Pauline reports. "'wait; we don't know what will happen.' Finally I gave in...thinking I would please her. I was wrong. She looked silently on the magnificent head of hair that had fallen into my hands, and, when I asked her what she was thinking she said, 'I think I am happy for having made this sacrifice for Jesus. I was eager to give Him my hair...' (She) had tears in her eyes."[18]

Thérèse's long blond hair was never discarded, a measure of how strongly others felt attached to those childhood curls. Some loving hands preserved them; the curls can be seen today at the Lisieux Carmel.

*   *   *   *   *

Inside the Carmel Thérèse's self-discipline began in earnest. To harness her own strong will she determined to obey her superiors without question in every detail. Thus she ate the legendary piles of undigestible beans. Her Prioress was given to outbursts and, according to Sister Marie of the Trinity, to imposing "a legion of petty regulations which she repealed or changed according to her fancy, with the result that little attention was paid to them."[19] Except by Thérèse. She obeyed even thoughtless suggestions. Mother Marie de Gonzague instructed her when sitting on the floor on her heels to sit on her *right* heel. Comfort dictated occasional shifts to the left heel; and though the Carmel was lenient with regard to such an obviously whimsical suggestion, throughout her life Thérèse sat *only* on her right heel.[20]

[18]GCI, p. 516, ft. 2.
[19]TE, p. 246.
[20]TE, p. 231, and p. 246.

Through "mortifications" and "penances" the Carmelites
at set times punished their bodies. Thérèse was spared severe practices because of her age, but she embraced the mortifications allowed her. These practices appeared to be in the
same spirit as detachment from bodily comforts, but when a
pronged iron cross worn on her breast made her sick Thérèse
decided that extraordinary penances were not for her.[21]
While detachment remained for Thérèse an absolutely essential step in finding God, its practice demanded a clear understanding of what it was, and was not. Thérèse abandoned the
pronged cross. Within a year of entering the monastery she
learned that the benign sounding "detachment" cut sharper
and deeper than any nettles or prongs.

When her father was committed to a mental hospital Thérèse was not free to leave the monastery grounds even to pay
him a brief visit. To step out of the cloister would be to reject
the new life she had fought so hard to live. Had she left she
could not have affected the decision to institutionalize him,
for that lay with her Uncle; she was not needed to care for
him, for two of her sisters were ready to nurse him. The hurt
was multiplied: her father's suffering, her own isolation from
him, the stabs of the town gossip. With two daughters
already gone, the loss of the youngest child, it was said,
destroyed old Mr. Martin.[22] Such pressure can shake the
resolve of a strong adult, yet Thérèse's rediscovery of her
"strength of soul" had occurred only 2 years earlier and she
was still only 16.

When her father was institutionalized Thérèse was granted
a remarkable opportunity which became a test of her judgment about the practice of detachment. Normally a novice
was not free to speak personally at will; she spoke with her
superiors or in a common group in recreation. Due to Mr.
Martin's condition the *Rule* was relaxed and Thérèse was
free to skip the communal recreation. In her pain she could
finally turn again to Pauline. As if a thin beam of light

[21] ME, p. 186.
[22] GCI, p. 530, ft. 4.

focused on the scene in the parlor, Thérèse saw clearly that
nothing the sisters said could help their father. If the idea of
letting *nothing* interfere with one's peace were valid, if dying
to the self were necessary, why relax *The Rule* during this
crisis? Though her sisters stayed in the parlor, Thérèse did
not.

"After hearing painful news in the parlour, such as our
father's state of health," Pauline testified, "she did not hang
around to comfort herself by talking to us about it; she
returned immediately to whatever she should have been
doing in the community at the time."[23]
With a conscious effort of will Thérèse resisted the strong
natural pull to Pauline. Sister Aimée of Jesus, a nun hostile
to the Martin clan, noticed:

"I saw her at recreation then, when her sisters were absent,
and she spoke to us perfectly calmly though the big tears in
her eyes showed us that she was not indeed unmoved by
these sufferings."[24]

*   *   *   *   *

At age 17 Thérèse discovered the writings of St. John of
the Cross, and for the next two years she read little else.[25]
Like Thomas à Kempis, John stresses active detachment
from all that is not Christ. He describes in *Ascent of Mount
Carmel* and *The Dark Night* how one passes through a purging both of the senses and of the spirit to reach "nakedness of
spirit."[26] First the soul actively purges itself of attachments
to any material thing and sensual appetite that competes
with the life of the spirit. Then starts an active purgation of
the spirit—the "journey in faith." "All inordinate feelings"
are purged; intellect, memory, will are purged.[27] After the
purging, the soul passes into the Dark Night—first the Night

[23]TE, p. 37.
[24]TE, p. 279.
[25]A, p. 179, and GC, ft. 18, p. 634.
[26]CWJC, p. 72.
[27]CWJC, pp. 62-3.

of Sense then the Night of Spirit. During the "stripping of the old man" one renounces all that is not God; but empty of human attachments and not yet filled with God one feels abandoned, alone in a dark night. John builds no easy path to spiritual union with God. He counsels strictness with oneself in small matters.

"By the very fact that a spiritual person rejoices in something and gives reign to the appetite in trifles, his rapport with God is darkened and his intellect clouded. This is what the divine Spirit teaches in the Book of Wisdom: *Contact with vanity and trifles, and the use of them, obscures good things, and the inconstancy of the appetite overturns and perverts the sense and judgment that is without malice.*"[28]

If one reads only these counsels John appears kin to the puritan who sees evil lurking in the most innocent objects and pleasures, evil in a pretty blue hat. But this is only a surface impression. For he does not speak of evil in things themselves, but cautions against *dependence* on things, *attachment* to anything that weighs down the spirit. He does not preach self-punishment but insists that one must shed the enemies of peace—anxiety, guilt, fear. John was no gloomy puritan. He was a Castilian whose poetry vibrates with sensual imagery, with images used as metaphors for the spiritual experience that ordinary language failed to convey. And his poetry exudes an appealing Spanish flavor.

To understand Thérèse's reason for the strict detachment she practiced, no better framework exists than John of the Cross's *Spiritual Canticle*, a poem of forty stanzas drawn from the Old Testament *Song of Songs*. The Old Testament dialogue between bride and bridegroom becomes a love song between the soul (the bride), and Christ (the Bridegroom). In translation the following selected stanzas lose John's colorful rhyming but retain the powerful tone of love:

[28]CWJC, p. 243. (Quoted from *Wisdom* 4:12)

Bride...

Where have you hidden,
Beloved, and left me moaning?
You fled like the stag
After wounding me;
I went out calling You, and You were gone.

Shepherds, you that go
Up through the sheepfolds to the hill,
If by chance you see
Him I love most,
Tell Him that I sicken, suffer, and die.

Seeking my Love
I will head for the mountains and for watersides,
I will not gather flowers,
Nor fear wild beasts;
I will go beyond strong men and frontiers.[29]

The bride in this poem is not punishing herself. Flowers
are not evil. The bride "will not gather flowers" because she
is consumed with love; with the lover's singlemindedness she
cares for nothing but the bridegroom.

Bride...

Catch us the foxes,
For our vineyard is now in flower,
While we fashion a cone of roses
Intricate as the pine's;
And let no one appear on the hill
...

Bridegroom...

Swift-winged birds,
Lions, stags and leaping roes,
Mountains, lowlands, and river banks,
Waters, winds and ardors
Watching fears of night:

[29]CWJC, p. 410.

By the pleasant lyres
And the siren's song, I conjure you
To cease your anger
And not touch the wall,
That the bride may sleep in deeper peace.
. . .

Beneath the apple tree:
There I took you for My own,
There I offered you My hand,
And there I restored you,
Where your mother was corrupted.
. . .

Bride. . .

In the inner wine cellar
I drank of my Beloved, and, when I went abroad
Through all this valley
I no longer knew anything,
And lost the herd which I was following.

There He gave me His breast;
There He taught me a sweet and living knowledge;
And I gave myself to Him,
Keeping nothing back;
There I promised to be His bride.

Now I occupy my soul
And all my energy in His service;
I no longer tend the herd,
Nor have I any other work
Now that my every act is love.

If, then, I am no longer
Seen or found on the common,
You will say that I am lost;
That, stricken by love,
I lost myself, and was found.
Bridegroom. . .

> She lived in solitude,
> And now in solitude has built her nest;
> And in solitude He guides her,
> He alone, Who also bears
> In solitude the wound of love.[30]
>
> . . .

To enter fully into a deep, spiritual love one must first be purged of the "corruption of the mother"—human nature, and freed from the distractions that erode love. "Catch us the foxes. . . Lions, stags, leaping roes. . . waters, winds and ardors, watching fears of the night. . . I conjure you to cease your anger and not touch the wall, That the bride may sleep in deeper peace."

Thérèse's practice of detaching herself from all things that were not God cut to the core of her own emotional reactions, other people's ideas of her—both critical and flattering, dependence on her sisters, even an attachment to any religious practice. Her habit of detachment remained strict, incisive and all-inclusive; but it was not an end in itself. "Stricken by love," writes John, "I lost myself, and was found."

*   *   *   *   *

When Céline Martin arrived at the Carmel 6½ years after Thérèse she found someone quite changed from the 13 year old who cried when she forgot a bunch of flowers for her mother's grave. Thérèse practiced detachment in the extreme. As did all Carmelites, Céline believed in the principle. Like many modern people, however, the sisters in the monastery were seldom rigid about minor rules.[31] Depending on interpretation one might term them either lax or flexible. Except for Thérèse.

"I could not overemphasize the point," wrote Céline in her *Memoirs*, ". . .(Thérèse) kept nothing which she did not absolutely need and she always cast far from her anything

[30]CWJC, pp. 412-14.
[31]TE, pp. 231 and 246.

that merely catered to convenience."[32] "She never showed any concern about her appearance or whether she was wearing a habit that fitted her or not. Her clothes, and even her hempen sandals were mended or patched until they were threadbare."[33] This change in Thérèse so struck Céline that she reported in her own memoirs incidents illustrating Thérèse's new strictness with herself.

"A novice... rubbed linseed oil over the cheap finish of her cell *ecritoire* (writing table), but... Thérèse had her scrub it with a brush until every trace of the oil had disappeared."[34] Thérèse's oil lamp was a monastery joke. It had a defective wick that she dug out and raised with a pin each time it was lit. She even scraped off the gold gilt from her prayer books. Occasionally Céline noticed signs of an internal struggle in her sister's face. Once Céline stained Thérèse's large hour glass which the nuns used to tell time. The sand glass was marred permanently; it took an "effort" for Thérèse to conceal her reaction.[35]

"By nature she was artistic," explains Céline, "and preferred objects that were attractive and in good taste."[36]

As a novice assigned to Thérèse for training[37] Céline learned that Thérèse's detaching herself from "possessions" cut far deeper than an hour glass. To Thérèse her vow of poverty meant she did not own her own time. As her poems became popular to celebrate the sisters' feast days she was often asked to write one but given no time for the task. She composed poetry in her head while doing her work as portress or laundress. With no free time until eight in the evening Thérèse nonetheless waited until then to jot down the

[32] ME, pp. 163-4.

[33] ME, p. 162.

[34] ME, p. 163.

[35] ME, pp. 162-4.

[36] ME, p. 162.

[37] From 1893 on Thérèse served as Assistant Mistress of Novices under Mother Marie de Gonzague as Director of Novices. Her duty, assigned by Pauline as Prioress, was to diplomatically blunt the effect of the former Prioress' authority. In effect, Thérèse was serving as Novice Mistress without the title.

lines that came to her in the morning. Sometimes she found it hard to remember the lines.[38] Never did she take time to make copies of her poems for herself.[39]

Thérèse believed she did not own even her own thoughts. From time to time in the narrow circle of convent life a peculiar and common form of "theft", as Thérèse called it, occurred: the theft of another's insight or idea, repeated in the gathering of the sisters without credit to the source. Good with words, Thérèse had thoughts "borrowed" and repeated without recognition. Such trifles can stir fury in the heart of one capable of heroic sacrifice.[40] Thérèse recognized this reaction as possessive, another threat to her peace. About three months before she died she wrote,

"...Jesus has given me the grace of not being any more attached to the goods of the mind and heart than to those of earth." Her thoughts, she explained, came from the Holy Spirit. "If I think this inspiration belongs to me, I would be like 'the donkey carrying the relics' who believed the reverence paid to the saints was being directed to him."[41]

Thérèse warned constantly against preoccupation with the self. She pointed out hidden ways in which the obsession with one's self intruded, such as excessive introspection, a pitfall of life in a community concerned with carving out "faults" to achieve "perfection." Constant dissection of one's thoughts and behavior was simply another form of preoccupation with the self.

"This tendency to fall back on self makes the soul barren..." Thérèse told Céline. The remedy for introspection? Works of charity.[42]

The impulse to justify oneself in the face of blame was another such hidden concern with the self. Thérèse describes tussling with another novice at the door to the Prioress'

[38] ME, p. 157.
[39] TE, p. 148.
[40] For Céline's view on this point see ME, p. 11.
[41] C, pp. 233-4.
[42] ME, p. 132.

bedroom over who should hand in the keys. Mother Marie de Gonzague awoke, Thérèse's rival blamed her, and Thérèse fled the room battling to control the impulse to defend herself.

"I told myself that if I began to justify myself I would not be able to retain my peace of soul..."[43]

Another trap was the desire for consolation in prayer. Thérèse believed that all desires for consolation, even in prayer, must be shed. We will examine this view more completely in a later chapter.

Life in a community knitted together for survival, as in a family, contains one other hidden snare. Often members assume the right to complain, to air petty angers and frustrations to one they trust, one expected to sympathize. Thérèse viewed such confiding as a self-indulgence, a hidden crutch to retard the inner life and a wedge disrupting the peace of the shared life. Sister Marie of the Trinity, an unstable young woman handed over to Thérèse for training, reports,

"One day when I was crying, and Sister Thérèse told me I should try to accustom myself to not showing my little sufferings, she added that nothing contributed so much to making community life depressing as emotional ups and downs."[44]

"She told us" reports Céline, "that in a community one must strive to be self-sufficient..."[45]

To Thérèse detachment meant a continuous resistance to clinging to things, people, emotions, impulses, ideas, habits, preoccupations, with the end of changing from the strong-willed, self-centered child she had been, and growing in the life of the spirit. Thérèse, quite simply, did not trust her "self." She did not shed her old identity as the little queen at great cost to attach herself to a new one, Thérèse the Carmelite, with a new set of possessions to cling to, however few they were. In a place where the subtle hazards of attachment

[43]C, 224.
[44]TE, p. 244.
[45]TE, p. 135.

went generally unrecognized, her strict practice of detachment was a lonely one.

"Virtue seemed to come so naturally to her that people thought she was inundated with consolations," testified Sister Teresa of St. Augustine, the nun who never guessed Thérèse's natural aversion to her. "I heard one sister say: 'Sister Thérèse gets no merit for practising virtue; she has never had to struggle for it.'"[46]

In the tradition of John of the Cross Thérèse taught Céline to "lean on nothing." When Céline envied her sister's skill at quoting scripture passages from memory Thérèse told her,

". . . To lean on such things is like leaning on a piece of red hot iron. It will always leave its little scar. We must lean on *nothing* even in the case of those things which. . . might help us in the spiritual life. . ."[47]

* * * * *

"I didn't come to Carmel to live with my sisters. . ." she wrote her last summer. "Ah! I really felt in advance that this living with one's own sisters had to be the cause of continual suffering when one wishes to grant nothing to one's natural inclinations."[48] Yet the final summer Thérèse was thrust again into their arms—with Céline as her nurse, and Pauline by her bedside, the barriers provided by the *Rule* leveled.

To dislodge herself from the image that Marie, Pauline and Céline held of her, to dislodge herself from her own habit of turning to them throughout childhood, and at the same time to show them love was a central struggle in Thérèse. She wanted, in fact, to live apart from her family, unknown. As late as the autumn before she died she hoped for transfer to a mission in Hanoi to live in a remote place where no one knew her.[49] Yet her autobiography is filled

---

[46]TE, p. 196.

[47]ME, pp. 32-3.

[48]C, p. 216.

[49]DE, p. 31. See also C, pp. 216-17.

with loving sentiments, warm memories and delight in her family.

"I don't understand the saints who don't love their family..." she said four months before she died.[50]

There is no contradiction. Thérèse fought to tamp down the habits that often pass for love: Céline's desire to spend recreations together as confidants; Marie's effort to mother Thérèse during the early days in Carmel; any assumption that Thérèse should side with her Pauline in the acute political rivalry for the office of Prioress. And Thérèse had to conquer her natural impulse to confide in Pauline. This took a strong act of the will.

When they worked together in the refectory from 1889 to 1891 they were free to speak. Pauline obtained permission from the Prioress to confide her intimate thoughts to Thérèse. Thérèse listened, but did not ask the same permission for herself.[51] This reserve continued even when Pauline was Prioress, and Thérèse, like all the other nuns, was free to confide in her.

"When her sister was prioress..." reports Sister Teresa of St. Augustine,...(Sister Thérèse) never once went along during night silence to talk to her."[52]

By the final summer Thérèse had reached a state of abandonment of her own will. She felt confident enough now to ease her own strictness.

"I no longer felt the necessity of refusing all human consolations," she wrote Mother Marie de Gonzague, "for my soul is strengthened by him whom I wanted to love uniquely."[53] The day before Thérèse was carried down to the infirmary where she finally died she told Pauline,

"This saying of Job: 'Although he should kill me, I will trust in him' has fascinated me from my childhood. But it took me a long time before I was established in this degree of

[50]LA, pp. 46-7.
[51]DE, p. 474.
[52]TE, p. 196.
[53]C, p. 237.

abandonment. Now I am there; God has placed me there. He took me into his arms and placed me there."[54]

Her sisters were by no means "there." Céline wanted a particular picture of Thérèse after she died.

"You are still harassed by desires, aren't you?" Thérèse said.[55] They were indeed, and as tuberculosis spread through her their strongest desires were linked to Thérèse's death. Unlike their patient the Martin sisters each held fantasies about her dying moments. In the contrast between their reactions to Thérèse's death and her own reactions we see the fruit of her strict practice of detachment.

Pauline felt pained that she was no longer Prioress for Thérèse could not die in her arms. This privilege belonged to Pauline's rival, Mother Marie de Gonzague. Thérèse didn't mind.

"God allows himself to be represented by whomever he wills," Thérèse told Pauline... "But this is of no importance. With you as Prioress now, there would have been the human element... I'm happy to die in the arms of Mother Prioress because she represents God for me."[56]

Marie imagined angels coming with the Lord,[57] and Céline's fantasy centered on who would receive Thérèse's dying "look."

"If God leaves me free," Thérèse said a few days before she died, "It will be for Mother Prioress."[58]

Thérèse's behavior at the moment of her death suggests clear control of her will. By then she was a "skeleton," too slight and in too much pain to be held in anyone's arms. In Céline's description of Thérèse's death the coveted "last look" is central. Her sentimental, melodramatic language and her interpretation which is turned on herself, reveal the sharp contrast between Céline and Thérèse:

[54]LA, p. 77.
[55]ME, p. 161.
[56]LA, p. 104.
[57]LA, p. 134.
[58]LA, p. 229.

During her final agony, a few moments before she expired, I was passing a little piece of ice over her burning lips, and at this moment she lifted her eyes to me and looked at me with prophetic insistence. Her look was filled with tenderness, and there was in it a superhuman expression of encouragement and promise as though she were saying to me:

"Go, go! Céline, I shall be with you!"

Did God reveal to her the long and laborious career I was to carry out here on earth for her sake, and did He will through this look to console me in my exile? For the memory of that last look, so much desired by all and given to me, sustains me always. . .[59]

Céline did not quite grasp Thérèse's relentless battle against the intrusion of the self in everything, at all times. The next passage in Céline's own description suggests a different interpretation:

The community was in suspense in the presence of this great scene; but suddenly our dear little Saint lowered her eyes in search of Mother Prioress, who was kneeling by her side. . .[60]

While Céline was caught in her own emotional reaction to Thérèse's "look", Thérèse turned from her sister to give the actual "last look," to which the nuns attached so much importance, to Mother Marie de Gonzague, the Prioress.[61] Thérèse's final conscious act was one of detachment.

[59] *Ibid.*

[60] *Ibid.*

[61] In a letter written 10 days after Thérèse died Pauline says that Thérèse's last look was for the Holy Virgin. She is referring to Thérèse's staring up toward the statue after she was assumed to be dead. DE, p. 571.

III

Jesus

"...for little girls, very good, very sweet, very diligent today, the Holy Child in the crib reserves all kinds of divine caresses." [1]
Pauline to Thérèse (age 10)

"...to be the spouse of Jesus we *must* resemble Jesus, and Jesus is all bloody..." [2]
Thérèse (age 16) to Céline.

When Pauline Martin taught her youngest sister about *Le Seigneur*, The Lord, she picked a familiar image: flowers. As a child Thérèse loved the "sight of fields enameled with *cornflowers*..." [3] In France, flowers decorated not only the fields, but the neighborhoods, gardens, window boxes.

"This baby loves flowers so much," Pauline wrote her aunt when Thérèse was 6½ years old, "to listen to her, she's very soon going to pick all there are of lilies of the valley in the *jardin de l'Etoile*..." [4] Filtered through Pauline Jesus

[1] Pauline to Thérèse, LC 7, end of Dec. 1882 or Jan. 1883, GCI, p. 157.

[2] Thérèse to Céline, LT 87, Ap. 4, 1889, GCI, p. 553.

[3] A, p. 29.

[4] Pauline to Mme. Guérin, LD, June 4, 1879, GCI, p. 135.

became "little Jesus," the child in the crib, who, like Thérèse, loved flowers. What Pauline taught, Thérèse embraced.

"I was very proud of my two older sisters," Thérèse wrote at age 22, "but the one who was my *ideal* from childhood was Pauline."[5]

Despite the death of their mother Pauline created a warm, safe world for Thérèse, one which fit the image of the Child Jesus safe in his crib. But when Thérèse was 9½ Pauline herself disrupted that secure world. She left home, and Thérèse, to join the cloister. Abruptly Thérèse's innocent trust that her sister would always be hers was shattered.

"...I saw *my Pauline* behind the *grille*...I said in the depths of my heart 'Pauline is lost to me!'...Towards the end of the year, I began to have a constant headache..."[6]

Pauline's influence over Thérèse's thinking about Jesus continued through brief visits and particularly through letters. A striking quality of these letters is their heavy saccharine tone. Pauline failed to grasp the depth of Thérèse's wound:

"Darling...you're the little rosebud of the rosebush of my affections...how eager I am to see it open up to the very gentle Sun of the Child Jesus' Love!...when the bud has become a rose, I know where I'll place it, my dear rose..."[7]

Pauline was planting important metaphors in Thérèse's mind, metaphors which would shift and change and emerge later on in a purer form. When Thérèse travelled to Rome at age 14 Pauline introduced a new image of Jesus to make a particular point: whether or not the Holy Father gave her permission to enter Carmel at 15, Thérèse already belonged to Jesus. She was, wrote Pauline, "the Divine Child's toy."[8]

"When the Blessed Virgin noticed that her Darling was weeping, it was then that she quickly placed the mysterious ball in his hand, and he smiled immediately...on the dear

[5]A, p. 20.

[6]A, p. 60.

[7]Pauline to Thérèse, LC 5, Around Dec. 20, 1882, GCI, p. 154.

[8]Pauline to Thérèse LD, Nov. 8, 1887, GCI, p. 309.

ball was written this name; *Thérèsita of the Child Jesus...*
Fear nothing, for Jesus says to you...'Nobody will be able
to snatch you from my hands!'"[9] Pauline wrote a dialogue
between Thérèse and Jesus:

"Oh! how happy I am! How I love my little ball! I can
pierce it; I can do all I want with it and always it repeats;
'Jesus, I love You! Jesus I love You.' To rejoice, to suffer, to
suffer again! All that You will, my dear little Jesus.'"[10]

In the same letter in which she injected the image of the
toy, Pauline used another metaphor:

"Yes, the bonds are already formed between Jesus and His
little Thérèse; Jesus is already Thérèse's Fiancé and Thérèse
the fiancée of Jesus. To suffer a little before the nuptials is
not asking too much!..."[11] To refer to Thérèse as a "fiancée" at age 14 seems discordant with the childish image of
the ball, but it was not new to Thérèse even then. She was
first referred to as "His little fiancée" when she was 9 years
old and lonesome for Pauline. Mother Marie de Gonzague,
the Prioress, wrote Thérèse to comfort her, to urge her to
eat. Like Pauline, Thérèse too, "...will become a good and
fervent *Spouse of Jesus!*"[12]

The idea of Jesus as her Fiancé took firmer root on the
night of Thérèse's first Communion at age 11. That evening
at the Carmel Pauline took her final vows:

"...I saw my *Pauline* who had become the spouse of
Jesus; I saw her with her white veil, one like mine, and her
crown of roses...I hoped to be with her soon and to await
heaven with her!"[13]

At age 16 Thérèse herself became the bride, and received a
wedding gift:

"Anticipating the desires of His fiancée, He gave her snow.
Snow! What mortal bridegroom, no matter how powerful

[9]Pauline to Thérèse LC 57, Nov. 9, 1887, GCI, p. 312. (See footnote on p. 336).

[10]Pauline to Thérèse LC 66, Nov. 23, 1887, GCI, p. 358.

[11]Pauline to Thérèse, LD, Nov. 8, 1887, GCI, pp. 309-10.

[12]Mother Marie de Gonzague to Thérèse, LC 6, End of Dec. 1882 or Jan. 1883,
GCI, p. 156.

[13]A, p. 78.

he may be, could make snow fall from heaven to charm his beloved.?"[14] A year and a half later when Thérèse pronounced her vows for life her marriage to Jesus was complete.

Though Thérèse absorbed the symbols given to her, an important difference developed between the way those around her used symbolic words and what these words meant to Thérèse. In Pauline's dialogue between Thérèse and Jesus, for example, the "ball" pleased Jesus. But Pauline used the image to preach a lesson: Thérèse should accept Jesus' will, whatever that may be.

When Thérèse explained the metaphor of the ball in her book of memories she didn't lock it into a lesson so much as play with the idea; Thérèse drew meaning *from* the ball. In her hands the metaphor is less sentimental, sharper, clearer:

> I had offered myself, for some time now, to the Child Jesus as his *little plaything.* I told him not to use me as a valuable toy children are content to look at but dare not touch, but to use me like a little ball of no value which He could throw on the ground, push with His foot, *pierce,* leave in a corner, or press to His heart if it pleased Him; in a word, I wanted to *amuse little Jesus,* to give Him pleasure; I wanted to give myself up to His *childish whims.* He heard my prayer.
>
> At Rome, Jesus pierced his little plaything... He let His little ball fall to the ground and He went off to sleep.[15]

Though nuns commonly considered Jesus their spouse, the word could easily remain abstract, evoking ideals of "loyalty," "devotion," "acceptance of his will." Thérèse did not react to symbols through such learned patterns. She was *marrying* Jesus. In a startlingly literal way she explored what that meant. Her cousin Jeanne Guérin was to be married within a week of Thérèse's ceremony and Thérèse observed how Jeanne treated her future husband.

[14]A, pp. 155-6.
[15]A, p. 136.

"It would be impossible dear Mother," she wrote Pauline, "for me to tell you how much I learned from her example concerning the delicate attentions a bride can bestow upon her bridegroom. I listened eagerly to what she was saying so that I would learn all I could since I didn't want to do less for my beloved Jesus than Jeanne did for her Francis..."[16] For fun Thérèse even wrote out an invitation:

> God Almighty, Creator of Heaven and Earth, Sovereign Ruler of the Universe, and the Most Glorious Virgin Mary, Queen of the Heavenly Court, announce to you the Spiritual Espousals of Their August Son, Jesus, King of kings, and Lord of lords, with little Thérèse Martin...
>
> Monsieur Louis Martin...and Madame Martin...wish to have you take part in the Marriage of their Daughter, Thérèse, with Jesus, the Word of God, the Second Person of the Adorable Trinity, who through the operation of the Holy Spirit was made man and Son of Mary, Queen of Heaven...[17]

The child in the crib remained a powerful image of Jesus throughout Thérèse's childhood. But Sister Thérèse of the Child Jesus, as she was known in the convent, was growing up—now she was his bride. Her literal reaction to the metaphor of the Spouse, her playing with this idea received in childhood, was preparing the ground for the intimate view to come.

* * * * *

While Thérèse was still a novice a shift occurred in the way she thought of Jesus: she focused on his face. Pauline showed her a picture, a cameo of the bearded face of the suffering Christ imprinted on a veil.[18] This face of Christ was

[16]A, p. 168.

[17]*Ibid.*

[18]GCI, p. 520, ft. 2. The devotion came from the writings of Sister Marie de Saint-Pierre of the Tours Carmel. Some confusion exists on the identification of the Face which Thérèse revered because of a painting based on the Shroud done by Céline after Thérèse had died, called The Face of Christ of the Carmel of Lisieux. Recent correspondence with the Carmel confirms that Thérèse never saw the Face on the Shroud.

not taken from The Shroud of Turin (which was little known and held suspect in the 19th century); it is more mannered, the features less rough and wounded. But the likeness and stark front view resemble that on the Shroud: both focus on the battered face with eyes closed. Once she had seen it Thérèse became devoted to "the Face of Our Spouse."[19] The day of her bridal ceremony at age 16 she changed her name. To "Thérèse of the Child Jesus" she added in a signature, "and the Holy Face."[20]

Within weeks of the ceremony the idea of suffering assumed a new meaning. She was not permitted even to say goodbye to her gentle father before he was whisked out of town and committed to a mental institution. Except for a very brief visit when he finally came home to Lisieux three years after that day, Thérèse remained cut off from him for the rest of his life.[21] The Innocent Victim was no longer so distant, and the meaning of Jesus' suffering face sharpened.

"To be the spouse of Jesus," she writes her sister Céline, "we *must* resemble Jesus, and Jesus is all bloody. . . Look at His eyes lifeless and lowered! Look at His wounds. . . Look at Jesus in His Face. . ."[22]

In a long flowing letter to Céline a year and a half later, just before her final vows, Thérèse copies out passage after passage from scripture. She begins with one from the book of Isaiah which was read in the Carmel's lenten services.[23] The fourth song of the Suffering Servant describes the appearance of the coming Messiah and for Thérèse was a critical discovery:

> Who would believe what we have heard? To whom has the arm of the Lord been revealed? The Christ will grow up like a sapling before the Lord and like a shoot that comes from parched soil. He is without beauty and with-

[19]A p. 152.

[20]GCI, p. 520, ft. 2.

[21]See Patricia O'Connor, *Thérèse of Lisieux:A Biography,* (Huntington, Indiana, 1983), pp. 70, 71 and 86.

[22]Thérèse to Céline, LT 87, April 4, 1889, GC, p. 553.

[23]GCI, p. 633, ft. 13.

out stately bearing; we have seen him; he had nothing that
would attract our eyes and we despised him. He appeared
to us as an object of scorn, the least of men, a man of
sorrows, acquainted with suffering!... His face is as
though hidden... He seemed to be despicable and we did
not recognize him.... He truly took our infirmities upon
himself, and he was burdened with our offenses. We
looked upon him as a leper, as a man struck by God and
humbled!... And yet he was pierced for our iniquities, he
was broken for our crimes. The chastisement which was
to procure our peace fell upon him, and we were healed
by his wounds.[24]

By age 17 Thérèse actively selects the imagery that speaks
most keenly to her and juxtaposes it with her new experience
of suffering: Louis Martin hidden away in a bed in the huge
mental hospital. In the same letter in which she quotes to
Céline Isaiah's whole passage on the scorned and broken
Messiah, she writes:

"Céline, since Jesus was alone in treading the wine which
He is giving us to drink, let us not refuse in our turn to wear
clothing stained in blood..."[25] Thérèse also quotes in that
letter from *The Canticle of Canticles,* the poetry of John of
the Cross, and *The Apocalypse.* Limited to reading fragments of the scriptures available in the community such as
communal prayers and readings, like an artist Thérèse noti-
ces details and phrases that echo each other. Though the
passages and images that she absorbed include those planted
by Pauline in her childhood, with the shock of Louis's mental illness and her discovery of Isaiah's Suffering Servant,
Thérèse no longer depends on Pauline.

*   *   *   *   *

When the priest murmured the words of consecration
over the thin wafer at Mass Thérèse believed that it became
the living Christ. The Eucharist, then, was an encounter with

[24]Isaiah 53:1-5, quoted in Thérèse to Céline, LT 108, July 18, 1890, GCI, p. 631.
[25]*Ibid.*

Jesus; but the reverence surrounding it conveyed awe rather than intimacy.

Mass at the Carmel was early in the morning. Thérèse sat in a stall fixed to the wall which faced into the center of the nuns' choir; during Mass her right side was toward the wall-sized iron grate that separated the nuns from the altar. On days chosen by the Prioress and chaplain[26] each veiled nun approached the right corner of the iron grate near Thérèse's wood stall, knelt, and the priest's hand passed the host through the opened porthole onto the waiting tongue.

Nothing else in Thérèse's experience approached the reverence given the Eucharist. A red lamp burned at all times in the sanctuary to indicate the consecrated host, and in the presence of the Tabernacle one kept silent. During the Mass the priest turned his back to the people, bending over the unseen host at the moment of the consecrating words whispered in Latin. As he slowly raised the host above his head most of the kneeling faithful cast their eyes down. Bells sounded the solemn moment. During the Mass no woman knelt in the sanctuary. If the priest required assistance it was given by a man or a boy. A woman might, as Thérèse did, cut the thin sheets of unleavened bread into wafers for the priest to consecrate. A woman might, as Thérèse did, clean and prepare the altar and the sacred vessels for the Mass. But a woman never knowingly touched even the smallest particle of the Sacred Host.

Only in the context of this deep reverence and distance does an incident that occurred a few months after Louis Martin's breakdown seem to set Thérèse's reaction to Jesus in the Eucharist apart from that of the other nuns. She and another novice were sweeping the public chapel. According to her companion,

[26]Stephane-Joseph Piat, O.F.M.,*Thérèse de Lisieux a la Decouverte de la Voie d'Enfance* (Paris: 1964), p. 78. After 1891 Superiors no longer officially controlled who should receive Holy Communion. In practice, however, Mother Marie de Gonzague's habits were retained in the Carmel of Lisieux. Summarium, p. 167.

"(Thérèse)...went and knelt at the altar, knocked at the door of the Tabernacle, and said, 'Are you there, Jesus, answer me, I beg You.'"[27]

To Thérèse Jesus was not only The Lord to whom one owed the most solemn reverence, but a living person inviting an intimate union. The Eucharist was her opportunity for the most direct encounter with Him. Four years before she entered the Carmel Thérèse had already experienced the Eucharist as a bonding. Of her First Communion at age 11 she wrote:

> ...I *felt* that I *was loved*, and I said, "I love You, and I give myself to You forever!" There were no demands made, no struggles, no sacrifices; for a long time now Jesus and poor little Thérèse *looked at* and understood each other. That day it was no longer simply a *look*, it was a fusion; they were no longer two. Thérèse had vanished as a drop of water is lost in the immensity of the ocean. Jesus alone remained....[28]

She passed afternoons at the Abbey School in the chapel in front of the Tabernacle, "for was not Jesus my *only Friend?* I knew how to speak only to Him..."[29]

Inside the Carmel, emotion linked to the Eucharist did not continue.

"I can't say that I frequently received consolation when making my thanksgivings after Mass; perhaps it is the time when I received the least."[30] The lack of emotion failed to worry Thérèse. The Eucharist remained Christ, real and alive; she prepared with a little imagination:

> I have offered myself to Jesus not as one desirous of her own consolation in His visit but simply to please Him

---

[27]GCI, p. 571. (Quoted from the Apostolic Process, 1915-16, testimony of Sister Martha of Jesus, p. 1273).

[28]A, p. 77.

[29]A, p. 87. Thérèse returned to the Abbey in the afternoons to qualify for the Children of Mary.

[30]A, p. 172.

who is giving Himself to me. When I am preparing for Holy Communion, I picture my soul as a piece of land and I beg the Blessed Virgin to remove from it *any rubbish* that would prevent it from being *free;* then I ask her to set up a huge tent worthy of *heaven*, adorning it with *her own* jewelry; finally, I invite all the angels and saints to come and conduct a magnificent concert there. It seems to me that when Jesus descends into my heart He is content to find Himself so well received and I, too, am content."[31]

As in the case of Thérèse's marriage to Jesus, her view of him in the Eucharist resembles a genuine human relationship far more than was customary in her day. In her era Catholics remained suspicious of familiarity: even within the Carmel daily Communion was not allowed.[32] As Thérèse thought about the Eucharist after kneeling at Mass so many mornings without permission to receive the sacrament, she concluded that, this restriction was wrong. Daily contact with Jesus in the Eucharist was not to be avoided, but sought.

"It is not to remain in a golden ciborium that he comes to us *each day* from heaven..."[33] she wrote in her memories.

A day came when Thérèse could no longer receive the Eucharist at all. In the final stages of tuberculosis she often choked and vomited and realized the risk that she would vomit up the Host. According to Pauline, her sisters, thinking that she craved the Eucharist, "insisted that she receive Communion."[34] But on the 20th of August, 1897, Pauline saw that Thérèse feared the risk.

"...That day she was unable to restrain herself any longer and she fell into tears...the choking produced by her sobs was so violent that, not only was she unable to answer us, but she made a sign to us not to say a word, not even to look

[31]*Ibid.*
[32]See footnote #26.
[33]A, p. 104.
[34]LA, p. 157, footnote.

at her. . . Never had I seen her in such agony."[35] Forty days later Thérèse died without ever again receiving the Eucharist.

Though Thérèse craved the encounter with Jesus in the Eucharist daily she did not continue to grieve over it. She did not equate the loss of the Eucharist with the loss of Christ. In June of that summer Thérèse had told Pauline not to be troubled if she came in one morning and found her dead without benefit of the sacraments.

"Everything," she said, "is grace."[36] Barred from daily communion, Thérèse believed that Jesus' life within her was not limited to the sacrament. Two years before she died, in her offering of herself to God she had asked a daring favor:

". . . I cannot receive Holy Communion as often as I desire, but, Lord, are you not *all-powerful?* Remain in me as in a tabernacle. ."[37] Such an intimate request was so foreign to the thinking of her time that one of the tribunal members in 1910 asked Pauline "if these words about 'real presence between one communion and the next. . .' were meant in some metaphorical sense or were they to be taken literally."

"I am certain," answered Pauline, "she meant them literally."[38]

*   *   *   *   *

Formal prayers to Jesus hinged on images less warmly human than majestic and distant, even the following excerpts from the Litany of the Most Sacred Heart of Jesus and the Litany of the Holy Name of Jesus:

> Heart of Jesus, Tabernacle of the Most High
> Heart of Jesus, House of God and Gate of heaven
> Heart of Jesus, Sacred Temple of God

[35] *Ibid.* She received Communion for the last time the day before this episode, on August 19.

[36] DE, June 5, No. 4, pp. 221.

[37] SS, p. 276.

[38] TE, p. 46.

Jesus, Brightness of eternal Light
Jesus, King of Glory
Jesus, Sun of Justice[39]

The mechanical chant of the litany suggested the worship of the Divine Being from afar, not a lone person speaking one to one.

Thérèse spoke to Jesus as a living person. Just a year before she died Thérèse wrote a long letter to her sister Marie in which she addressed Jesus in a style overflowing with feeling and warmth:

> O Jesus, allow me in my boundless gratitude to say to You that Your *love reaches unto folly*. In the presence of this folly how can you not desire that my heart leap towards You? How can my confidence, then, have any limits? Ah! the saints have committed their *follies* for You, and they have done great things because they are eagles.
>
> Jesus, I am too little to perform great actions, and my own *folly* is this: to trust that Your Love will accept me as a victim. My *folly* consists in begging the eagles, my brothers, to obtain for me the favor of flying towards the Sun of Love with the *Divine Eagle's own wings!*[40]

These images may echo the litanies but the tone is distinctly familiar: Jesus is not a distant Being to Thérèse. Her tone is as personal as the *Song of Songs*, as the poetry of John of the Cross. One reads words that Thérèse underlined two and three times pouring out her feeling to Jesus, calling Him Sun and Eagle and Beacon and "*my first and only Friend*, you whom I *love* UNIQUELY,"[41] as if reading an intimate love letter.   ✗

Here lies the problem in Thérèse's sisters explaining her to others. Pauline and Marie and Céline did not easily grasp the freshness of Thérèse's view, imbued as they were with the

[39]*St. Joseph Daily Missal*, (New York 1959), p. 1302, 1303.
[40]B, 200.
[41]B, 197.

pious, remote tradition in prayer and the well-worn formal imagery such as appeared in the litanies. Nor did they grasp how distinct her religious experience was from their own notions of it gleaned from lives of the saints. Throughout her last summer Thérèse resisted her sisters' interpretations of what Jesus meant to her.

For Marie the ultimate experience at death would be a vision of Jesus. Eight weeks before Thérèse's death Marie stood by her bed in the infirmary, a small room looking out on the courtyard. A hot Thursday in August, Thérèse was exhausted and soaked with perspiration from a night of pain and nightmares. Marie tried to comfort her little sister with familiar pieties. At her death, Marie said, Thérèse would see "angels. . . resplendent with light and beauty," coming with the Lord.

"All these images do me no good," Thérèse said. "I can nourish myself on nothing but the truth. This is why I've never wanted any visions. . ."[42]

Thérèse did not think like her sister Marie; she avoided conventional pious phrases.

". . .conversations with creatures, even pious conversations, fatigued my soul," she wrote in her memories of childhood. "I felt it was far more valuable to speak to God than to speak about Him, for there is so much self-love intermingled with spiritual conversations!"[43] Thérèse recoiled from creating a haze of artificial mystery. To interpret religious symbols too strictly—as in the case of Marie's angels coming with the Lord—trivialized the real mystery.

"We can't see," Thérèse said with regard to Marie's prediction of seeing Jesus and angels at her death, "here on earth, heaven, the angels. . .just as they are. I prefer to wait until after my death."[44]

Even Pauline who managed to glimpse the uniqueness of Thérèse's inner life fitted her sister's comments and descriptions into familiar categories. Six days before Thérèse died

[42]LA, p. 134.
[43]A, p. 87.
[44]LA, p. 134.

Pauline asked her if she had any "intuition" about what day it would be. Pauline's question betrays another conventional viewpoint: if Thérèse were gifted with remarkable religious insight, must she not also know such practical information as the date of her own death?

"...I know nothing except what you know," Thérèse told Pauline. "I understand nothing except through what I see and feel..."[45] The dates of future events were not among the favors granted to Thérèse, nor did they interest her.

The question arises whether Thérèse's words as filtered through Pauline are always Thérèse's literal words or sometimes Pauline's interpretation. In the case of Thérèse's religious experience the question concerns ecstasy. In July of that final summer Pauline was trying to get the record straight on a number of details. She asked Thérèse to describe what happened when she offered herself to God's love. According to Pauline Thérèse answered:

> ...I was seized with such a violent love for God that I can't explain it except by saying it felt as though I were totally plunged into fire. Oh! What fire and what sweetness at one and the same time! I was on fire with love, and I felt that one minute more, one second more, and I wouldn't be able to sustain this ardor without dying. I understood then, what the saints were saying about these states which they experienced so often. As for me, I experienced it only once and for one single instant..."[46]

When Thérèse described the same experience in her own book of memories she had written simply:

"...you know the rivers or rather the oceans of graces which flooded my soul. Ah! Since that happy day it seems to me that *Love* penetrates and surrounds me..."[47] And that was all. No mention of any extraordinary experience, any ecstasy occuring during the following week.

[45]LA, p. 199.
[46]LA, p. 77.
[47]A, p. 181.

An oral tradition in the convent maintained that Thérèse reported the intense experience to Pauline (as Prioress) when it happened; the report disturbed Pauline so much that Thérèse omitted it from her memories.[48] But considering the marked difference in style between the words Pauline reported and Thérèse's usual manner of speaking or writing, Jean-Francois Six suggests that Pauline interpreted Thérèse's experience in terms more appropriate to St. Teresa of Avila, the great mystic of her order.[49] Though Pauline tended to report events reliably, she often took liberties with Thérèse's wording[50] and tended to reduce Thérèse's descriptions to a recognizable formula. On the question of her experience of Jesus, as in all other questions, we are safer to stay with Thérèse's firmly authenticated words and to avoid too much interpretation. When Thérèse writes of her own inner life, as with a completed poem, her meaning is distilled to it s core.

Three months before she died Thérèse wrote the section of her memories centered most on her religious life. Here we glimpse a little of what her union with Jesus meant to her. She explains the passage from the *Song of Songs, "Draw me, we shall run:"*

> ..."*No man can come after me, unless the FATHER who sent me draw him,*" Jesus has said...
>
> What is it then to ask to be "*Drawn*" if not to be united in an intimate way to the object which captivates our heart? If fire and iron had the use of reason, and if the latter said to the other, "Draw Me," would it not prove that it desires to be identified with the fire in such a way that the fire penetrate and drink it up with its burning substance and seem to become one with it?...this is my prayer...I ask Jesus to draw me into the flames of His love, to unite me so closely to Him that He live and act in me...[51]

---

[48]DE, 7.7.2, p. 456.

[49]Jean-François Six, *Thérèse of Lisieux, au Carmel,* (Paris, 1973), pp. 216-17.

[50]See O'Connor, *Thérèse of Lisieux, A Biography,* pp. 145-6.

[51]C, p. 257.

IV

The Romantic—The Martyr

> "I felt born within my heart a *great desire* to suffer..."[1]
> Thérèse, (age 11)

> "My desires for martyrdom *are nothing*. It is not they that give me the limitless confidence I feel in my heart."[2]
> Thérèse, (age 23)

By the time Thérèse was born every educated person in France knew the name Gustave Flaubert. Sixteen years before Thérèse's birth Flaubert shocked the French public with a novel about the impact of romantic dreams on a well-reared, intelligent provincial woman. Flaubert saw danger in the Romantic tendency to indulge one's own emotions, to elevate one's own suffering soul, to live for untested ideas.

Thérèse Martin grew up in Flaubert's Normandy. Like many a young girl she believed herself made for an imagined life more heroic than that of a middle class woman in an ordinary French town. But Thérèse possessed a critical mind and consistently put her ideas to the test of experience.

[1]A p. 79.
[2]Thérèse to Marie, LT 197, CGII, Sept. 17, 1896, p. 894.

While still in school she learned not to expect her fulfillment from the attention or love of another person.

"One of my friends was obliged to go back to her family and she returned. . .a few months later. During her absence, I *had thought about her*, treasuring a little ring she had given me. When I saw my companion back again my joy was great, but all I received from her was a cold glance. My love was not understood. I felt this and I did not *beg* for an affection that was refused. . ."[3] Thérèse wrote these lines two years before her death. She wrote, too, that she continued to love that child. But this rejection held a sharp lesson: it was the last time she risked herself to an intimate friendship outside of her family.

"A too ardent love of creatures," she decided, was an "empoisoned cup."[4] "With a heart such as mine, I would have allowed myself to be taken and my wings to be clipped, and then how would I have been able to *fly and be at rest?*. . .I know that without Him, I could have fallen as low as St. Mary Magdalene. . ."[5]

Lonely in school, Thérèse dreamed of a future in which she and Pauline would be hermits together in a far-off desert. Like any fantasy, Thérèse's desert was idealized. When she and her cousin Marie played at being hermits they had "a little garden where they grew corn and other vegetables." The desert of Thérèse's fancy was a haven from people, a haven from school, and a place where her loving "second mother" would be all hers.[6]

Accidentally she overheard Pauline talking of her plans to join the cloister.

> ". . .I understood that Pauline was going to leave me to enter a convent. I understood, too, she *would not wait for me* and I was about to lose my second *Mother!* Ah! how can I express the anguish of my heart! In one instant, I

[3]A, p. 82.

[4]A, p. 83.

[5]A, p. 83 (Quoted from Psalm 54:7).

[6]A, pp. 54 & 57.

understood what life was; until then, I had never seen it so sad; but it appeared to me in all its reality, and I saw it as nothing but a continual suffering and separation. . ."[7]

Failed by the person she trusted most, Thérèse turned her dreams away from human relationships to imagined glory. Like many another young French girl she was stirred by the story of Joan of Arc:

> When reading the accounts of the patriotic deeds of French heroines, especially the *Venerable* JOAN OF ARC, I had a great desire to imitate them; and it seemed I felt within me the same burning zeal with which they were animated. . . I considered that I was born for *glory* and when I searched out the means of attaining it, God . . . made me understand my own *glory* would not be evident to the eyes of mortals, that it would consist in becoming a great *saint!*. . . I didn't think then that one had to suffer very much to reach sanctity. . .[8]

The romantic emotion merged with an imagined ideal: feeling a "burning zeal" that she thought must be what the heroines felt, she believed herself, too, to be "born for glory." But her childish dream concealed a flaw:

"I didn't think then that one had to suffer very much to reach sanctity. . ."

By the time Thérèse reached the age of 11 the idea of suffering had blended with the dream of glory and was glazed with the same emotions. When she wrote her childhood memories at age 22 she recalled the day after her First Communion:

"I felt born within my heart a *great desire* to suffer. . . suffering became my attraction; it had charms about it which ravished me without my understanding them very well. . ."[9]

Thérèse had suffered as a child but it was essentially an

[7]A, p. 58.

[8]A, p. 72.

[9]A, p. 79.

interior suffering—the pain of loss, of abandonment, of isolation. With little direct experience of physical pain Thérèse
fixed a "great desire" on "suffering," an abstraction.

On her trip to Rome at the age of 14 the ideal of martyrdom took concrete shape in the form of a "tiny bit of pavement marked with a cross." Inflamed with excitement, Thérèse said, she and Céline "...threw ourselves on our knees
on this sacred soil...My heart was beating hard when my
lips touched the dust stained with the blood of the first
Christians. I asked for the grace of being a martyr for Jesus
and felt that my prayer was answered!"[10] But the pavement
and dust of the Coliseum were far distant from a real person
tortured to death. Thérèse dreamed of a glorious death as a
14 year old boy dreams of the death of a hero in battle, with
an imagination too sheltered from experience to paint in the
real details.

Thérèse fastened her dreams of glory, martyrdom, suffering on a single tangible place—the Carmel of Lisieux. In one
sense it was not exotic or remote at all, this set of stone
buildings sitting on a little crescent street in the center of her
own home town. But these buildings housed Pauline and
Marie and 24 other women who lived a mysterious life of
dramatic sacrifice hidden away from the eyes of the town.
All Thérèse could see of them from the public chapel were
dark veils behind a huge double grille. These silent women
lived for high ideals: to atone for others' sins and to contemplate God. And Thérèse would "sacrifice" herself too. But
there was much young emotion still mingled with this sacra-
fice. A year after she joined the Carmelites Thérèse was as
excited as any bride; on her "wedding" day everything thrilled
her. Louis was "so handsome, so *dignified*." "Nothing was
missing, not even the snow!...the monastery garden was
white like me!"[11] Innocent delight. Thérèse was unaware that
the concrete face of "suffering" with its terrible human details
was about to enter her life.

* * * * *

[10] A, p. 131.
[11] A, p. 154, 155.

In her written memories Thérèse said emphatically that nothing surprised her about the cloistered life.

"I found the religious life to be *exactly* as I had imagined it, no sacrifice astonished me..."[12] She imagined the discipline, the prayer, the fasting rather well. But she certainly never imagined the form her real suffering would take. Two months after she entered the convent her father abruptly disappeared for several days.[13] The episode upset Thérèse. She faced it as a "first trial" of suffering, "but I feel I can still bear greater trials."[14] The following winter, a month after her bridal ceremony her father hallucinated and picked up a gun to defend his household. He was slipped out of town quickly to the mental institution where he spent the next three years.[15]

"...that day," Thérèse later wrote, "I didn't say I was able to suffer more!"[16] That she considered Louis' breakdown the start of the suffering she had vaguely and excitedly anticipated is clear from a letter to Céline:

"The *Martydom* is beginning. Let us enter the arena together..."[17] Céline and Thérèse had been raised together, held long conversations on religion together at home, and together they had leaped down to kiss the Coliseum floor. But at this point we can see the beginning of a sharp divergence between Thérèse's changed view and Céline's continuing romantic attitude. Céline wrote to Thérèse:

"If you only knew what I dreamt the other night! You had just died a martyr; a man had taken you into the woods to kill you. With envy, I saw you leave for martyrdom...suddenly we saw a light smoke arising to heaven, and then a bird sang. We said to ourselves: the sacrifice is accomplished! Thérèse is a martyr...My heart leaped at this news:

[12]A, p. 149.

[13]See O'Connor, pp. 65-66.

[14]A, p. 156.

[15]See O'Connor, pp. 65-67.

[16]A, p. 157.

[17]Thérèse to Céline, LT 82, Feb. 28, 1889, GCI, p. 537.

And what about me!..." Excitedly, she described a boy
tearing out her own eyes.[18]

Thérèse wrote back a kind letter to Céline. She shifted the
focus to a plain image of martyrdom, one that already
reflects at age 16 her grasp of how ordinary, undramatic and
lonely human suffering really is.

It might happen that way, Thérèse wrote. "...in the
meanwhile, let us begin our martyrdom, let Jesus *tear* from
us all that is most dear to us...Before dying by the sword,
let us die by pinpricks..."[19] What about the "burning zeal"
she felt when she read of Joan of Arc?

"...Let us suffer in peace!" Thérèse wrote Céline. "...the
one who says *peace* is not saying joy, or at least *felt* joy...to
suffer in peace it is enough to will all that Jesus wills...to be
the spouse of Jesus we *must* resemble Jesus, and Jesus is all
bloody..."[20] When she kissed the dust of the Coliseum
floor Thérèse's heart had beat hard with excitement; after
her father's breakdown, never again would she connect "felt
joy" with martyrdom. To Thérèse the word martyrdom was
now linked neither with excitement nor with public glory.
The martyr became her father: shy, quiet, a gentle man who
loved to take walks and to fish and to recite poetry while
rocking Thérèse on his lap, a man innocent of evil or even
unkindness—lying in a bed in a 500 patient mental hospital
covering his head with his handkerchief.[21]

Like Jesus, Louis Martin was an innocent victim whose
suffering saved others. "He was broken for our crimes."
"The chastisement which was to procure our peace fell upon
him, and we were healed by his wounds."[22] These words of
Isaiah were among those Thérèse copied out for Céline during the summer of 1890. Redemption, another abstract word

[18]Céline to Thérèse, LC 110, March 13, 1889, GCI, p. 549.

[19]Thérèse to Céline, LT 86, March 15, 1889, GCI, p. 552.

[20]Thérèse to Céline, LT 87, April 4, 1889, GCI, p. 553.

[21]TE, p. 154.

[22]Thérèse to Céline, LT 108, July 18, 1890, GCI, p. 631.

which Thérèse had heard over and over again, had taken on a very concrete meaning.

Human emotion, human glory had vanished from martyrdom. Yet a residue of that old image remained, for only the *worldly* glory faded from Thérèse's dream.

"...already God *sees us in glory*, He TAKES DELIGHT in *our eternal beatitude!* Ah! what good this does my soul, and I understand now why He is not bargaining with us..."23

At this stage Thérèse believed without a whisper of doubt that martyrdom, especially hidden martyrdom, would one day have its reward.

"...Ah, here is great Love," she wrote Céline, "to love Jesus without feeling the sweetness of his love...this is martyrdom...Well, then, *let us die as martyrs*...Unknown martyrdom, known to God alone,...a martyrdom without honor, without triumph...That is love pushed to the point of heroism...But, one day, a grateful God will cry out: 'Now, my turn.' Oh, what will we see then?..."24

* * * * *

One need not search far into the Old Testament to find echoes of the rite of human sacrifice. Given a son in his old age, Abraham was asked to sacrifice that child. He had bound Isaac to the wood, stretched out his hand and seized the knife to kill his son (Genesis 22:10) before the ram appeared to take his child's place. In the Jewish tradition the animal took the place of the human offering; the animal was a symbol.

By Jesus' time the offering of animals was so routine the ritual was drained of its symbolic power. Jesus cut through the formalism of paying money for a priest to offer a lamb or turtledoves to God. Killing animals to offer him was not what God wanted. His own death pierced to the heart of the ritual: God wanted each of us in a free offering. Thus the

23Thérèse to Céline, LT 108, July 18, 1890, GCI, p. 630.

24Thérèse to Céline, LT 94, July 14, 1889, GCI, p. 557.

eating of Jesus' body and blood is central to Christianity. In place of the blood offerings of animals each Christian becomes one with Jesus, each Christian is willing to die to the self that reflects any fad, or thought, or dream, or instinct, or emotion, or cultural good that shuts out God.

This point of view was sharply at odds with the bourgeois ethic all around the Martins, the ethic that tried to own, to possess—one belonged to a family and inherited this house, this money, this name. One went to great lengths to provide comfort for the family members, to help them along to the best education possible, to nurture their talent. Externally the Martins were middle class—with a large brick home, a garden, toys, attractive dresses and educational and travel opportunities for the girls. What set them apart from many other Christian families is that the Martins took this idea of offering a life to God not as an outmoded residue of the Medieval Church, but quite literally. As one after the other of his daughters asked to leave home to join the cloister Louis Martin consciously made a gift of each of his children to God. A friend commented to Louis after Thérèse left home,

"Abraham did not outdo you. You would have done as he did, if God had asked you to sacrifice your little Queen." Louis said,

"Yes, but I own I should have raised my knife slowly, hoping for the angel and the ram!"[25] Thus, only a few weeks after Louis had offered her to God in the Carmel chapel, Thérèse understood that it was now *her* turn. Louis was the Victim; she must surrender him.

Viewing Louis as the new Victim prepared the ground for Thérèse's formal offering of herself to God in June of 1895 at the age of 22. Clearly she considered this act distinct from the offering she had already made of her life to God as a Carmelite nun. She wrote out the words, obtained permission from her Prioress, then she read the offering in a small room adjoining her cell with only Céline as witness. Though

[25]Quoted in Stephane-Joseph Piat, O.F.M., *The Story of a Family*, (New York, 1948), p. 370.

Thérèse's offering turns on the word Love it contains a request for martyrdom:

"In order to live in one single act of perfect Love, I OFFER MYSELF AS A VICTIM OF HOLOCAUST TO YOUR MERCIFUL LOVE, asking You to consume me incessantly, allowing the waves of *infinite tenderness* shut up within You to overflow into my soul, and that thus I may become a *martyr* of Your *Love*, o my God!

May this martyrdom, after having prepared me to appear before You, finally cause me to die..."[26]

What is Thérèse asking? A literal reading of the text suggests that she wants to die like the historical martyrs. But all three of her sisters insisted in later years that she meant something else.

Céline Martin emphasized in her own memoirs that Thérèse was not requesting suffering.

"The new state of victim she proposed was *martyrdom* indeed, but a *martyrdom of love*...she did not identify the martyrdom of love with that call to suffering which distinguishes the victims of God's justice."[27] Marie Martin agreed. Thérèse urged this offering on all those about her. One day while Marie was raking grass Thérèse suggested that she make this act of Love. Marie refused; she dreaded pain. "Besides," she told Thérèse that day, "the word *victim* has always repelled me." But Marie finally changed her mind and always maintained that Thérèse would not have urged on her a request for suffering.[28]

Years later the Liturgical Office of Saint Thérèse contained the words: "...*inflamed with the desire of suffering,* she offered herself...as a victim to the merciful love of God." The wording disturbed Pauline enough that she lobbied with the Sacred Congregation of Rites to change this text. In 1932 she succeeded. The words "inflamed with the

---

[26]SS, p. 277.

[27]ME, p. 80.

[28]ME, pp. 90-91.

desire of suffering" were changed to "...*on fire with divine love*..."[29]

And Thérèse wrote the same sentiment in her copybook the very year that she offered herself to God:

"My childish desires have all flown away...Neither do I desire any longer suffering or death, and still I love them both; it is *love* alone that attracts me...I desired them for a long time; I possessed suffering and believed I had touched the shores of heaven...Now, abandonment alone guides me. I have no other compass! I can no longer ask for anything with fervor except the accomplishment of God's will in my soul..."[30]

As her life drew to a close it appears that Thérèse no longer craved suffering itself. The idea of suffering for God was just another of those attachments to be dropped in favor of abandoning herself to whatever God wanted of her. But the year before she died she addressed a letter to Jesus which she sent to her sister Marie, containing her girlish dreams to die a martyr's death. Since by 1896 when she wrote the letter Thérèse no longer dealt in such abstractions but in very concrete images, these dreams too, took definite shape.

"*Martyrdom* was the dream of my youth, and this dream has grown with me within Carmel's cloisters. But here again, I feel that my dream is a folly, for I cannot confine myself to desiring *one kind* of martyrdom. To satisfy me I need *all*...I would be scourged and crucified. I would die flayed like St. Bartholomew. I would be plunged into boiling oil like St. John..."[31]

Buried for life within a small enclosure in a modest French town, this fantasy of a dramatic death was indeed, as she knew, a folly.

"During my meditation, my desires caused me a veritable martyrdom..." Then it was that Thérèse opened the Epistle of St. Paul to the Corinthians, right to the famous pas-

---

[29] ME, p. 85.

[30] A, p. 178.

[31] B, p. 193.

sages on charity. St. Paul's words galvanized all her desires and clarified for her the purpose of her own undramatic life.

"...*Charity* gave me the key to my *vocation*...I understood that LOVE COMPRISED ALL VOCATIONS, THAT LOVE WAS EVERYTHING, THAT IT EMBRACED ALL TIMES AND PLACES...IN A WORD, THAT IT WAS ETERNAL!

...I cried out:...my *vocation*, at last I have found it...MY VOCATION IS LOVE!"[32]

Thérèse stated clearly that her vocation was love, *not* martyrdom. Still, when one reads the words "I would be scourged and crucified. I would die flayed...I would be plunged into boiling oil..." It is easy to sympathize with her sister Marie's reaction. She glossed over the section on love to rivet her attention on these words.

"...I am seized with a certain sadness in your extraordinary desire for martyrdom. That is indeed the proof of your love. Yes, love you do possess: but not I!...I fear all that you love. That...is a proof that I do not love Jesus as you do.

Ah! you say that you do nothing, that you are a poor miserable little bird, but what about your desires? How do you reckon them? The good God certainly regards them as works..."[33] Marie missed the critical shift in Thérèse's focus. With so much official attention on martyrdom and suffering and self-sacrifice, Marie still believed Thérèse sought the martyr's death and glory, desired the martyr's crown. Martyrdom *had* claimed a central place in Thérèse's notion of self-sacrifice: the romantic lover who will die for love. While the idea of martyrdom was not wholly effaced, it had shifted to the background. Love became central. As with an optical illusion, the field had reversed but Marie continued to see the old pattern.

"My *desires* for martyrdom are *nothing*," Thérèse wrote back to her sister to clarify her point. "It is not they that give

[32]B, pp. 193, 4.

[33]Marie to Thérèse, Sept. 16, 1896, CL, p. 287.

me the limitless confidence I feel in my heart. They are, in truth, the spiritual riches which *make* us *unjust*—when we rest in them complacently and think they are *something grand...*" To stress her point Thérèse quoted Jesus' words in Gethsemane as he recoiled from the suffering he faced:

"...Jesus said: 'Father, take this chalice from me.' ...after that how can you say that my desires are the mark of my love?..."[34]

* * * * *

Thérèse's first bad fit of coughing came in the dark. Since the candle was doused and she would not disobey the smallest rule she did not see the blood until morning. All that year Thérèse continued the monastic schedule. The next winter she fasted during most of Lent and slept on her straw mattress in her unheated cell. By April she was severely ill and in mid-May was relieved of her duties. Her death was quite as gruesome as any martyr's death. The tubercles soften the lung tissue until it grows spongy and bloody, the patient gasps for air, has the sensation of suffocating, coughs up blood, endures high fevers, and as the disease spreads to other parts of the body, great pain. She died in September 1897, eight and one half years after she entered the chapel on her father's arm dressed as bride.

The suffering did not surprise her, nor did she see it as an answer to a request.

"Fortunately I did not ask God for suffering," she told her cousin Marie Guérin. "If I had, I would be afraid of not having enough patience to bear it. But since it comes solely from God, he cannot refuse me the grace and patience I need for it."[35]

Thérèse believed one must be "ground down through suffering to become the wheat of God,"[36] but the suffering was neither to prove love nor for her own glory.

[34]Thérèse to Marie, LT 197, Sept. 17, 1896, CGII, pp. 894-5.

[35]Marie Guérin to Isidore Guérin, August 27, 1897, LA, p. 290.

[36]LA, p. 144.

"Suffering joined to Love," she wrote two months before she died, "is . . . the only thing that appears to me desirable in this vale of tears."[37] By the time she was dying from tuberculosis this attitude converged with another to provide a distinctive perspective. Thérèse no longer linked suffering to her own image, reward, proof of love, or glory, in this world or the next. She linked suffering to redeeming others, and to the acceptance of whatever God wanted of her. In mid-June she told Pauline:

". . . What anyone says to me about death no longer penetrates; it slides over me as it would over smooth glass. It's finished! The hope of death is all used up. Undoubtedly, God does not will that I think of it as I did before I became sick. At that time, this thought was necessary for me and very profitable; I really felt it. But today it's just the contrary. God wills that I abandon myself like a very little child who is not disturbed by what others will do to him."[38]

Thérèse's purging of all imaginative fancy about her future seems complete. She is now indifferent to whether she lives or dies. The critical word is *now*.

"Now I want to be sick all my life if that gives pleasure to God. . ." As the editors of *Derniers Entretiens* point out, "now" recurs obviously in Thérèse's writing of those last years.[39] In French the word receives more stress than in English. *Maintenant* is more clearly a word deliberately chosen rather than one merely tacked on to a thought. In the past Thérèse had dreamed; *now* she lives in each moment. "I'm like a little child, very little", she told Pauline a month before she died. "I'm without any thought, I suffer from minute to minute."[40]

Thérèse's changed attitude toward suffering and death appears in sharp relief against Pauline's. As Pauline sat hour

---

[37]Thérèse to Abbè Bellière, LT 253, July 13, 1897, CGII, p. 1027.

[38]LA, p. 65.

[39]I am indebted to *Derniers Entretiens* for this insight. On p. 43. a number of examples of Thérèse's stressed use *maintenant* are cited.

[40]LA, p. 170.

by hour alongside Thérèse's bed in the hot infirmary that last summer she was building toward an expected drama.

"You will probably die on July 16, the feast of Our Lady of Mount Carmel, or on August 6, the feast of the Holy Face," Pauline suggested early in the summer.

"Eat 'dates' as much as you want," quipped her patient. "I myself no longer want to eat any...I have been too much taken in by dates."[41] One day early in September Thérèse told Pauline that the thought of dying left her calm.

"I'm very happy, but I can't say that I am experiencing a living joy and transports of happiness, no!"

"You prefer to die rather than to live?" Pauline suggested, and Thérèse quickly realized her sister was fishing for an attitude she'd read about in Teresa of Avila.

✓ "O little Mother," Thérèse said, "I don't love one thing more than another; I could not say like our holy Mother St. Teresa 'I die because I cannot die.' What God prefers and chooses for me, that is what pleases me more."[42] By this time Pauline was thinking of Thérèse as a saint. Observing her closely with her own ideas of sainthood in mind, she anticipated for Thérèse the "death of Love" which John of the Cross described in The *Living Flame of Love.*

> O living flame of love
> that tenderly wounds my soul
> in its deepest center!
> . . .
> O sweet cautery,
> O delightful wound!
> O gentle hand! O delicate touch
> . . .
> In killing you changed death to life.[43]

John explained his meaning:

---

[41]LA, p. 83.

[42]LA, p. 183.

[43]CWJC, pp. 578-9.

> It should be known that the death of persons who have
> reached this state is far different in its cause and mode
> than the death of others, even though it is similar in its
> natural circumstances. If the death of other people is
> caused by sickness or old age, the death of these persons is
> not so induced, in spite of their being sick or old; their
> soul is not wrested from them unless by some impetus and
> encounter of love far more sublime than previous ones, of
> greater power, and more valiant, since it tears through
> this veil and carries off the jewel, which is the soul.
>
> The death of such persons is very gentle and very sweet,
> sweeter and more gentle than was their whole spiritual life
> on earth. For they die with the most sublime impulses and
> delightful encounters of love.... [44]

But Thérèse was dying by inches. As week after week of the
hot summer dragged by she lay suffocating, choking, vomiting blood, slowly losing first the right lung, then the left.
Late August found her in such torment that Pauline believed
tuberculosis had invaded her intestines:

> She was no longer able to perform bodily functions
> except with terrible pains. If we placed her in a seated
> position to ease the suffocation after a long coughing
> spell, she thought she was sitting "on iron spikes." She
> begged prayers because, she said, the pain was enough "to
> make her lose her reason." She asked that we not leave
> poisonous medicines for external use within her reach
> ... Besides, she added, if she hadn't any faith, she would
> not have hesitated for one instant to take her life. [45]

Thérèse's agony and temptation to suicide bore no resem-
blance to John of the Cross's description of the death of Love.
This baffled Pauline, but not Thérèse. She was 24 now and
had read John of the Cross very little since the age of 18.
Since then she had read, almost exclusively, the Gospels.
Her idea of death came directly from Jesus.

[44]CWJC, pp. 571-2.

[45]LA, pp. 162-3. (footnote)

"Our Lord died on the Cross in agony," she told Pauline, "and yet this is the most beautiful death of love. This is the only one that was seen...to die of love is not to die in transports..."[46]

No longer did Thérèse idealize any dream, even about her own death. But Pauline did not know how to live like Thérèse, from minute to minute. Pauline was plagued with expectation.

Thérèse's death was witnessed by the entire community of nuns crowded round her bed. Sister Mary Magdalen of the Blessed Sacrament describes what happened:

"When called to her bedside with the rest of the community at the moment of her death, I saw...how she raised her head again when she seemed to be dead and stared up with a look of amazement and extreme happiness. I have often been present at nuns' deaths, but I have never seen anything like that."[47] Marie Guérin had time to rise from her knees, approach the bed, and pass a candle back and forth in front of Thérèse's eyes. Pauline said this state lasted "the space of a credo." But Pauline injected in her description the word ecstasy. As she had once before, again she described Thérèse's experience as if it were identical to that of Teresa of Avila.

"The sisters had time to kneel down around her bed, and they were witnesses to the ecstasy of the little, dying saint."[48]

The scholars who studied all the medical records and testimonies of Thérèse's last months to compile the French *Derniers Entretiens* (Last Conversations) questioned Pauline's account of Thérèse's "ecstasy." It was inspired, they note, by St. Teresa of Avila's *Life*.

"With the passage of time, the witnesses amplified their reports of this final ecstasy."[49] They cite a letter Pauline

[46]LA, p. 73.
[47]TE, p. 264.
[48]LA, p. 206.
[49]DE, pp. 570-71.

wrote only 10 days after the death in which the word does not appear.[50]

Pauline's interpretation of the moments when Thérèse was looking upward also echo words from St. John of the Cross:[51]

"She made certain beautiful movements with her head, as though someone had divinely wounded her with an arrow of love, then had withdrawn the arrow to wound her again..."[52]

What Thérèse experienced at the moment of her death cannot be known. But by the time of her death she attached no importance to either ecstasy or any other experience described by a saint or connected with the death of a saint. She didn't expect it, she didn't anticipate it, and she warned her sisters explicitly against looking for "anything extraordinary" at her death. By the end of her life Thérèse had no need to look to saints or to any imagined idea for guidelines. She identified completely with one person, Jesus—the spotless Victim who redeemed others by his act of Love and who died in agony. About three hours before her death—suffocating, completely conscious without morphine to relieve the pain, Thérèse said,

"Never would I have believed it was possible to suffer so much! Never! Never! I cannot explain this except by the ardent desires I have had to save souls."[53]

* * * * *

Years later Céline wrote in her own memoirs that in the convent she once complained to Thérèse that all her enthusiasm had dried up.

"'In the world,' I told her, 'I was so inflamed with zeal that ... I was willing to face wild beasts, and I yearned to travel

---

[50]*Ibid.*

[51]I refer again to the interpretation of Jean-Francois Six.

[52]LA, pp. 206-7.

[53]LA, p. 205.

to the ends of the earth...Whereas now...I have courage for nothing.'"

"That's a sign of youth," Thérèse told her. "...Those momentary ardours which impel us to go out and win the world to Christ—at the cost of every imaginable danger, ...only adds another touch of romance to our beautiful dreams. No, the courage that counts with God is that ...which Our Lord showed in the Garden of Olives: on the one hand, a natural desire to turn away from suffering; on the other, in anguish of soul, the willing acceptance of the chalice which his Father had sent him."[54]

Thérèse shed the romantic trappings of the feelings and images surrounding the glorious martyrdom of heroes. But she did not end up a bitter realist. Like Don Quixote she retained innocence and trust in the face of the brutal realities. Nor did she abandon the core of the heroic ideal of offering one's life to God, even to the point of dying. She merely lifted the ideal out of the realm of the remote, heroic legends, scraped it clean of gothic emotion and placed it squarely in the hands of the ordinary man and women. The girl who wanted to die the extraordinary death of a martyr died from tuberculosis, the most common death in Europe. And her commonplace death was quite alright with Thérèse, for glory and drama were no longer the point. With her fine sense of humor she did not miss the irony.

"And I who desired martyrdom," she quipped the month before she died, "is it possible that I should die in bed!"[55]

[54]ME, pp. 190-91.
[55]LA, p. 132.

V

Thérèse's Way

"She told me how she'd worn her little iron cross for a long time and that it made her sick. She told me, too, that it wasn't God's will for her, nor for us to throw ourselves into great mortifications..."[1]
Pauline Martin

"...I wanted to find an elevator to raise me to Jesus, for I am too small to climb the rough stairway of perfection..."[2]
Thérèse Martin

Like a piece of classical sculpture, Mother Marie de Gonzague stands at the center of Thérèse's training in the cloistered life. Father Stephane-Joseph Piat, who has written extensively on the Martin family, has described this woman who served as Thérèse's Prioress for six and a half years:

"Tall, gracious, sympathetic and willingly obliging, with something about her both naive and candid, Mother Marie de Gonzague exercised on all who approached her whether in the interior of the cloister or the parlor, a real gift of

[1]LA, p. 115.
[2]C, p. 207.

seduction. Without having superior intelligence, she had spirit, prestige, charm."[3] As she charmed others, she charmed Thérèse. By Thérèse's own admission, initially she idolized the Prioress. Toward the end of her life Thérèse described to Mother Marie de Gonzague

"...how I loved you and the sacrifices I was obliged to make at the commencement of my religious life in order not to become attached to you in a physical way as a dog is attached to its master..."[4]

Mother Marie de Gonzague was imbued with the common philosophy in religious communities of the time: "humiliations" strengthened the soul. According to the description of the Abbè Combes, the first scholar to win entrance to the full archives of the Carmel in the late 1940's, the "ideal of the Carmel" under this Prioress was such that "iron crosses and flagellations with nettles held great honor..."[5] *The Treasure of the Carmel,* a book defining the vocation of a Carmelite over the centuries, was heavy with words that justified the view of Mother Marie de Gonzague:

> ...the goal of the Order of the Carmel is to honor the incarnation and the humiliations of the Savior, and to unite oneself intimately to the Word made flesh, and to glorify God by imitating his hidden life, suffering and sacrifice.
>
> It is, further, to pray for sinners, to offer oneself for them to the divine justice, and to take their place, throughout the rigors of an austere and crucified life, with the penance that they have not done...a Carmelite is charged with continuing and completing in some manner the work of Jesus Christ's mediation...[6]

[3]Piat, *Thérèse de Lisieux a la decouverte de la voie d'enfance,* p. 81.

[4]C, p. 237.

[5]Abbè Combes, *Sainte Thérèse et sa Mission,* (Paris, 1954), quoted in Six, *Thérèse de Lisieux au Carmel,* p. 193.

[6]Quoted in Piat, o.f.m., *Thérèse de Lisieux a la decouverte de la voie d'enfance,* p. 78.

"The great mark of the vocation to our holy Order," states another text, "is the salutary fear of the judgments of God...."[7]

Thomas à Kempis, whose *Imitation of Christ* Thérèse virtually memorized before entering the Carmel, also described the rigors of God's justice.

"...It is better," wrote Thomas, "to purge our sins and root out our vices now, than to keep them for some future purgation...What else does this fire have to feed on but your sins? The more lenient you are on yourself and the more you yield to your flesh, the greater will be your future suffering, for you are only storing up fuel for the fire..."[8]

Mother Marie de Gonzague embodied, then, a familiar and widely held point of view. And she headed a community of women seeking to live the contemplative life. To root out human behavior labeled as "faults" and "weaknesses" by means of penance, fasting and humiliation was the road to "perfection." But the arduous "ascent of Mount Carmel" toward perfect self-mastery was mere prelude, for the aim of the contemplative nun was union with God. Mother Marie de Gonzague, however, valued the prelude.

"Suffering is a very great thing!" she said, as she suffered at the close of her own life. "It is through it that we prove to the good God our love and our gratitude."[9]

In this spirit Mother Marie de Gonzague denied permission for Thérèse to have injections of morphine in the last weeks of her life, even in the final hours which were so agonizing for Thérèse that Sister Marie of the Trinity left the sickroom because "I could no longer bear to assist at so painful a spectacle."[10] Yet that afternoon Mother Marie de Gonzague sat for hours by Thérèse's bed comforting her in the most endearing terms, calling her "my poor little one."[11]

[7]*Ibid.*
[8]IC, p. 686.
[9]DE, p. 556.
[10]TE, p. 255 (On the question of morphine see DE, p. 555.)
[11]LA, p. 205, 206.

Seven years later when the Prioress lay dying of cancer, she refused morphine for herself.[12] To judge Mother Marie de Gonzague as cruel or sadistic is to inject modern assumptions into an earlier time.

For Thérèse as a young novice, Mother Marie de Gonzague's narrow path to perfection seemed surely the way to God. And she genuinely preferred the severe discipline of the Prioress to the babying of her sister Marie.[13] But Thérèse struggled with the path to perfection. Slow at mending, unaccustomed to housework, at times even dozing off to sleep during Mass, her inability to carve out her "faults" tormented her. She who wanted to make a grand sacrifice of herself to God was never safe from the dread that she might offend God, even while praying.

"It is necessary to tremble every time we go to the choir to say the Office," warned the 17th century Jacques Gallement in the *Treasure of the Carmel.* "It is necessary to have a great reserve in the presence of God, for you must know there are no faults that God pardons less then those done in chanting his praises."[14] Sensitive, honest, Thérèse recognized faults in herself that others didn't even notice. With rigorous perfection out of her reach, Mother Marie de Gonzague's path to union with God plunged Thérèse into conflict.

Another nun in the Carmel attracted Thérèse's attention. From the day she first entered the community, Thérèse was drawn to the elderly nun, who was revered in the Carmel as its Foundress.

"The choir was in darkness," she wrote, ". . . and what struck me first were the eyes of our holy Mother Geneviève which were fixed on me. I remained kneeling for a moment at her feet, thanking God for the grace he gave me of knowing a saint, and then I followed Mother Marie de Gonzague into the different places of the community."[15] One day while

[12]DE, pp. 555-556.
[13]C, p. 206.
[14]Piat, *Thérèse de Lisieux a la decouverte de la voie d'enfance,* p. 79.
[15]A, p. 148.

she was in turmoil Thérèse went to visit Mother Geneviève who was in her eighties and in bed. With the limit of two visitors already in the room, Thérèse turned to leave. Mother Geneviève must have noticed signs of stress; she always had a word for Thérèse and this time she quoted St. Paul: "Serve God with *peace* and *joy*; remember, my child, *Our God is a God of Peace.*" Thérèse describes the impact Mother Geneviève's words made on her:

> After thanking her very simply, I left but was moved to the point of tears and was convinced that God had revealed the state of my soul to her. That day I had been severely tried even to the verge of sadness; I was in such a night that I no longer knew whether God loved me...
>
> The following Sunday, I wanted to know what revelation Mother Geneviève had received; she assured me she had received *none* at all, and then my admiration was greater still when I saw the degree to which Jesus was living within her and making her act and speak. Ah! that type of sanctity seems the *truest* and the *most holy* to me, and it is the type that I desire because in it one meets with no deceptions.[16]

Mother Geneviève's simplicity and trust also impressed Thérèse on another occasion.

"Mother," Thérèse said to her, "you will not go to purgatory!"

"I hope not," answered the elderly nun.

"Ah! surely." Thérèse later wrote, "God does not disappoint a trust so filled with humility..."[17] Within the Carmel

---

16 A, pp. 169-170.
17 A, p. 170.

In the late 1940's Maxence Van Der Meersch's interpretation of Thérèse's life as a rejection of the ideal of perfection sparked harsh reactions from theologians focused mainly on his unscholarly style and free interpretation of Thérèse's words. Van Der Meersch, a novelist, offended scholars by dramatizing the relationships between Thérèse and Mother Marie de Gonzague and Mother Geneviève, casting Mother Marie de Gonzague as a villain. Critics also attacked Van Der Meersch for summarizing Thérèse's sanctity in the phrase "know yourself." The controversy sank to ridicule and led some theologians to defend Thérèse's virtue and perfection

of Lisieux Thérèse had met a nun whom she considered a saint who approached God distinctly differently from the way of Mother Marie de Gonzague. With the passage of time Thérèse saw practices that she decided were not the will of God. Within the Carmel the spirit of unworthiness to approach the Lord accompanied the spirit of perfection. A recommendation dating from early in the 19th century urged the Prioress to restrict Holy Communion in the case of sisters "who believed themselves able to approach the sacraments with defects and external faults, frequent and habitual, such as infractions of silence, and humiliating and indiscreet words." [18] In practice the Prioress controlled who received the sacrament and how often; Mother Marie de Gonzague gave the permission arbitrarily once to reward a sister who trapped a rat. [19] Despite the rigorous fasting, penances, mortifications and humiliations, despite the nettles and the pronged crosses Mother Marie de Gonzague's devotion masked a quite human flaw: she failed to apply the practice of detachment within herself. An aristocrat among commoners, she never lost the sense of herself as the noble Marie-Adèle-Rosalie-Davy de Virville.

Aware of her own adolescent tendency to idolize the Prioress, Thérèse observed this in another young nun—Sister Martha of Jesus. Thérèse watched it, distrusted it, and saw the Prioress encourage it. Finally Thérèse risked offending the woman who held complete power over her by telling Sister Martha frankly that the Prioress was "doing your soul a great deal of harm." Such feelings in nuns were "poison." [20] The spirit of perfection failed to make Mother Marie de Gonzague a saint. Mother Geneviève, on the other hand,

against apparent attack. Van Der Meersch's insights regarding Mother Geneviève's impact on Thérèse were eclipsed by the battle, as was Thérèse's aversion to the ideal of perfection.

See Maxence Van Der Meersch, *La Petite Sainte Thérèse*, (Paris: Editions Albion Michel, 1947), and *La Petite Sainte Thérèse de Maxence Van Der Meersch Devant La Critique et Devant les Textes*. (Paris: Editions Saint-Paul, 1950).

[18] Piat, *Thérèse de Lisieux a la decouverte de la voie d'enfance*, p. 79.

[19] *Summarium*, p. 167.

[20] TE, p. 223.

was riveted neither on her own great penances nor on her own faults. Yet she did not fear, or even expect, Purgatory; her simple "I hope not" was built not on justice or a list of sacrifices, but on trust.

What finally convinced Thérèse that the path of perfection was not for her was an incident involving a pronged cross. Normally the Prioress denied the young Thérèse permission to use instruments of penance because of her age; but early in her monastery life Thérèse received permission to wear a pronged cross under her clothes directly on her chest. Pauline reports what happened:

"She told me that in her desire to suffer, one day she had thrust deeper into her flesh a small iron cross, which marked her and (the mark) stayed there for months, and that she made herself sick to the point of having to go to bed."[21] "She told me, too, that it wasn't God's will for her, nor for us to throw ourselves into great mortifications; this sickness was proof of it."[22] Thérèse warned Pauline of a hidden trap: "...the most austere penances can mingle very well with natural satisfactions."[23]

* * * * *

From Thérèse's earliest memories the word "little" had woven in and out of the Martin family correspondence and conversation. Everyone in the family was *"petite"*, not only "little Thérèse," but "little Céline" and even "little Father."[24] To her mother Thérèse was the "little imp."[25] "Little" was linked with another common word in Thérèse's life: child. In writing about the period of her life near her first Communion Thérèse reports:

"...(Marie) was speaking to me about suffering and she told me I would probably not walk that way, that God

[21] DE, p. 497.
[22] LA, p. 115.
[23] DE, p. 497.
[24] See, for example, LT 46, LT 47, LT 48, in GCI, pp. 421-24.
[25] Quoted in A, p. 17.

would always carry me as a child."[26] Being the child of the family gave Thérèse a certain license, even on the trip to Rome in the midst of a large pilgrimage of older men and women. At a "magnificent golden reliquary" containing a nail reputedly used to fasten Jesus to the cross, Thérèse "found a way of placing my *little finger* in one of the openings of the reliquary" and touched the nail. "Really I was far too brazen! Happily, God, who knows the depths of our hearts, was aware that my intention was pure... I was acting toward him like a *child* who believes everything is permitted and looks upon the treasures of its Father as its own."[27] On the same trip the 14 year old Thérèse quite consciously slipped inside the inner cloister of an Italian monastery where women were strictly forbidden.

"...all of a sudden I saw a good old Carmelite friar ...making a sign for me to leave. But instead of going, I approached him and showing him the cloister paintings I made a sign that they were very beautiful." Her excuse for violating the cloister?

"He undoubtedly understood by the way I wore my hair and from my youthful appearance that I was only a child, so he smiled at me and left. He saw he was not in the presence of an enemy."[28] A child is free to misbehave a bit; a child "looks upon the Treasures of its Father as its own."

To Thérèse the word "child" meant something distinct from the dependent, naive behavior suggested by the word "childish." She demonstrated clearly her own dislike for such behavior. At age 11 when Thérèse made a retreat away from home it embarrassed her to discover that she was the only girl there who didn't know how to comb her own hair.[29] During her final summer alive she told Pauline that Father Pichon, the priest she asked to be her spiritual director before entering Carmel, "...treated me too much as a

[26] A, p. 79.
[27] A, pp. 139-140.
[28] A, p. 140.
[29] A, p. 75.

child."[30] Father Pichon called her "the Benjamin," and when visiting her soon after she entered the Carmel told her her fervor was "childish" and her "way was very sweet."[31]

Quite distinct from Father Pichon's patronizing view of Thérèse as "childish" was her own sense of her true character. In her own written memories Thérèse quoted from a letter to Pauline written by her mother a few months before she died.

"The little one will be all right..." Zélie said, "she has a spirit about her which I have not seen in any of you."[32] Thérèse believed that she lost her strength of character when her mother died but regained it a week before her 14th birthday when she had the religious experience which jolted her free from prolonged turmoil: "...I found once again my *childhood* character, and entered more and more into the serious side of life."[33] Speaking of herself in the third person, Thérèse said she recovered "...the strength of soul which she had lost at the age of four and a half..."[34] But Thérèse would pass through another period of torment before her final realization of what her "childhood character" meant to her spiritually.

During the first three years in the Carmel Thérèse was plunged into new torment sparked by striving to root out her "faults" and her "weaknesses". Her inner conflict apparently came to a head in the fall of 1891. That year Thérèse went to confession to a retreat master named Father Alexis Prou.

> ...I felt disposed to say nothing of my interior dispositions since I didn't know how to express them, but I had hardly entered the confessional when I felt my soul expand. After speaking only a few words, I *was understood* in a marvelous way...He told me that *my faults*

[30]LA, p. 73.

[31]A, p. 149.

[32]A, p. 28. Quoted from a letter from Zélie Martin to Pauline, March 22, 1877.

[33]A, p. 34.

[34]A, p. 98.

> caused God no pain, and that holding as he did God's
> place, he was telling me in His name that God was very
> much pleased with me.
>   Oh! how happy I was to hear those consoling words!
> Never had I heard that our faults could not cause God
> any pain, and this assurance filled me with joy...[35]

That assurance never deserted her. "My nature was such that fear made me recoil; with *love* not only did I advance, I actually *flew*."[36] Freed from fear, certain that the way of dramatic penance and mortification was not for her, over the next three years Thérèse developed her own *way*. It allowed for the many differences in people, for the lives which the "Lord was pleased to caress...from the cradle to the grave...,"[37] for the "poor savages (who) died in great numbers without ever having heard the name of God pronounced."[38] Thérèse's way was not, in fact, unique, but involved a remarkably clear vision. She blended her perceptions about the strength of her childhood character, her distrust of the "natural satisfactions" contained in the austere tradition of Perfection, the simplicity of Mother Geneviève, and the references to littleness which she found in the scriptures, and expressed her insights to Pauline in the language they shared:

"...if all flowers wanted to be roses, nature would lose her springtime beauty, and the fields would no longer be decked out with little wild flowers. And so it is in the world of souls...."[39] Her analogy was meant to be precise: "...if all souls resembled those of the Holy Doctors who illumined the Church with the clarity of their teachings, it seems God would not descend so low when coming to their heart. But He created the child who knows only how to make his feeble cries heard; He has created the poor savage who has nothing

[35]A, pp. 173-4.
[36]A, p. 174.
[37]A, p. 14.
[38]*Ibid.*
[39]*Ibid.*

but the natural law to guide him. It is to their hearts that God deigns to lower Himself. These are the wild flowers whose simplicity attracts him."[40]

"Because I was little and weak," she writes, "He lowered Himself to me..."[41]

* * * * *

Thérèse's sisters understood that she was carving out a pathway to sanctity for ordinary people, one that side-stepped the "rough stairway of perfection." After her death they made persistent and sincere efforts to explain her way to a world raised on the philosophy of perfection. Her sisters' explanations were not wrong so much as oversimplified. Such an apparently simple idea can be misunderstood easily.

As a novice Céline had frequent contacts with her sister in the Carmel. To her Thérèse's way seemed to consist primarily in performing small but difficult acts such as not rubbing her hands together in the biting cold; it was also in performing little hidden kindnesses, a "little way." Céline who struggled against her own "petty reactions" to the irritating personalities about her noticed that no one was too irritating for Thérèse.

"It looked as if when someone was unpleasant to her, she became kinder, gentler and more considerate..."[42]

What Céline observed in Thérèse was true. But isolated, her examples can imply the distortion that Thérèse focused herself essentially on a continuous effort to perform little acts, as if small deeds should be judged superior to great deeds. As an incident described in her memories suggests, Thérèse mistrusted the attitude of judging on the basis of deeds at all. It was Christmas time. Recreation was rather dull when the sound of the portress bell rang out twice—the large outer gate must be opened to bring in trees for the crib. At that moment the sister in charge asked Thérèse or the nun

[40]*Ibid.*
[41]A, p. 105.
[42]TE, p. 132.

next to her if either wanted to serve as the third party required whenever the nuns opened the great gate. Suspecting that the nun alongside her wanted to go as much as she did, Thérèse untied her apron slowly to give her the chance. Thérèse tells the result:

"'Ah! I thought as much," said the nun in charge, "you were not going to gain this pearl for your crown, you were going too slowly.' Certainly the whole community believed I had acted through selfishness...This incident prevents me from being vain when I am judged favorably...Since one can take my little acts of virtue for imperfections, one can also be mistaken in taking for virtue what is nothing but imperfection."[43]

Thérèse turned away from gauging virtue, whether grand or small, in a manner that was fixed, static, away from judging what a person *is*. Deeds involved motivation, and motivation was too complex to judge. Her littleness was not centered in her acts but depended on something else:

"...'the way of man is not his own,'" she wrote to Céline, "and sometimes we surprise ourselves by wanting something that catches the eye...we must see ourselves as *little souls* which God must uphold from instant to instant..."[44] Her emphasis is not on little acts in themselves, but on grasping her own smallness, on recognizing her continuous need for God to uphold her.

Her point of view was not an easy one to nurture in a setting in which the sisters regularly judged each other's virtue. To follow confidently a path that diverged from what she was taught, a path distinct from what the other nuns noticed and respected, she had to free herself from concern over their approval. Indifference to unkind and even harsh judgments of her as slow and lazy was especially hard for the sole teenager among 26 older women more experienced in the Carmelite life.

In her earliest days in the convent Thérèse developed a strong desire to keep her inner life safe from the glare of

[43]C, pp. 221-2.
[44]Thérèse to Céline, June 7, 1897, CL, p. 342.

others, to keep "hidden." Her letters to Pauline in the first year contain frequent references to herself as the grain of sand.

". . . The grain of sand does not desire to be *humbled*; this is still too glorious since one would be obliged to be occupied with it. It desires only one thing, to be FORGOTTEN, counted for *nothing!*. . ."[45] At the end of her life Thérèse told Pauline the incident which taught her conclusively the folly of other's opinions. She was a novice when it happened.

"Sister St. Vincent de Paul saw me with Mother Prioress, and she exclaimed: 'Oh! how well she looks! Is this big girl strong! Is she plump!' I left, quite humbled by the compliment, when Sister Magdalene stopped me in front of the kitchen and said: 'But what is becoming of you, poor little Sister Thérèse of the Child Jesus! You are fading away before our eyes. If you continue at this pace, with an appearance that makes one tremble, you won't observe the Rule very long!' . . . ever since that moment I have never attached any importance to the opinion of creatures. . . reproaches and compliments glide over me without leaving the slightest imprint."[46]

Like Céline, Pauline also tried to explain her sister. Often Pauline relies on extracting phrases in the tradition of abstract religious writing and her attempt to clarify Thérèse's way hinges on the isolation of such a phrase: the Way of Spiritual Childhood. The editors of *Derniers Entretiens* concluded that this phrase appears to be Pauline's interpretation, for the evidence suggests that Thérèse never wrote these words herself.[47] The phrase appears for the first time in the 1907 edition of *Story of a Soul*,[48] an edition which Pauline

[45]Thérèse to Pauline, LT 95, July-Aug. (?), 1889, CG I, p. 580.

[46]LA, pp. 111-12.

[47]DE, p. 470.

Céline testified that Thérèse did not say "Spiritual Childhood." Quoted in Conrad de Meester, *Dynmaque de la Confiance,* (Paris: Cerf, 1969), p. 55. De Meester believes the phrase "spiritual childhood" expresses Thérèse's view accurately. Abbé Combes, the first scholar to examine the Carmel Archives, did not consider this phrase identical with Thérèse's "little way." See De Meester, pp. 57-58.

[48]*Ibid.* This phrase also appears in the last conversations with Thérèse which Pauline reported.

rewrote and edited extensively. In support of this view the editors cite the following exchange between Pauline and Thérèse appearing in the original edition of *Story of a Soul,* (1898) in which the phrase does not appear:

Pauline: "You seek always to resemble little children, but tell us in two words what must one do to possess the spirit of childhood? What is it to remain a child?" Thérèse: "To remain little, is to discover one's nothingness, it is to always await the good God, it is not to afflict oneself with one's faults. Finally, *it is to win no fortune, to be disquieted about nothing.*"[49]

"The Way of Spiritual Childhood" became the popularly quoted summation of Thérèse's path to God. Speaking about Thérèse in 1921, Pope Benedict XV said,

"In spiritual childhood is the secret of sanctity for all the faithful of the Catholic world."[50] Some time after the Pope's declaration a nun who had never known Thérèse was complaining to Pauline that the expression was inexact and lent itself to distortion. Pauline replied,

"But you know well that Thérèse never used it! It is mine."[51]

* * * * *

At Pauline's request, Mother Marie de Gonzague ordered Thérèse to write down her thoughts about life in the Carmel for a "circular," an obituary letter customarily sent to sister Carmels. Thérèse wrote propped up in a wheelchair in June 1897, less than four months before she died. Thérèse was devoted to obedience. She bowed silently to the Prioress's authority over her in every detail—from the choice of a physician in whom Thérèse had no faith,[52] to painful cauter-

---

[49]DE, p. 521.

[50]Quoted in SS, p. vii.

[51]Quoted in DE, p. 579.

[52]See, for example LA, pp. 71, 77, 78. There was a physician within the Martin family—Dr. Francis la Neele.

ization of her back with heated needles.[53] Now she must write for this proud woman her own insights which were contrary to Mother Marie de Gonzague's ideal of perfection. With simplicity, the 24 year old told her 63 year old Prioress the truth:

> Mother, you know yourself that those souls are rare who don't measure the divine power according to their own narrow minds;... For a very long time, I have known that this way of measuring experience according to years is practiced among human beings. For instance, the holy King David has sung to the Lord: *"I am YOUNG and despised."* And in the same Psalm 118, he does not hesitate to add: *"I have had understanding above old men, because I have sought your will. Your word is a lamp to my feet. I am prepared to carry out your commandments and I am TROUBLED ABOUT NOTHING."* ... I am *too little* to have any vanity now, I am *too little* to compose beautiful sentences in order to have you believe that I have a lot of humility. I prefer to agree very simply that the Almighty has done great things in the soul of his divine Mother's child, and the greatest thing is to have shown her her *littleness,* her impotence.[54]

The Lord, Thérèse explained, leads souls through different paths. Some saints refuse to leave anything of themselves behind, while others like St. Teresa of Avila, leave much writing.

"Which of these two types of saints is more pleasing to God? It seems to me, Mother, they are equally pleasing to Him since all of them followed the inspiration of the Holy Spirit..."[55] It is in the words written for Mother Marie de Gonzague, the disciple of mortification and perfection, that Thérèse stated most clearly her own Way, how she found it, and what it meant:

[53]ME, p. 214.
[54]C, pp. 209, 10.
[55]C, p. 207.

You know, Mother, I have always wanted to be a saint. Alas! I have always noticed that when I compared myself to the saints, there is between them and me the same difference that exists between a mountain whose summit is lost in the clouds and the obscure grain of sand trampled underfoot by the passers-by. Instead of becoming discouraged, I said to myself: God cannot inspire unrealizable desires. I can, then, in spite of my littleness, aspire to holiness. It is impossible for me to grow up, and so I must bear with myself such as I am with all my imperfections. But I want to seek out a means of going to heaven by a little way, a way that is very straight, very short, and totally new.

We are living now in an age of inventions, and we no longer have to take the trouble of climbing stairs, for in the homes of the rich, an elevator has replaced these...I wanted to find an elevator which would raise me to Jesus, for I am too small to climb the rough stairway of perfection. I searched, then, in the Scriptures for some sign of this elevator, the object of my desires, and I read these words coming from the mouth of Eternal Wisdom: *"Whoever is a LITTLE ONE, let him come to me."*...But wanting to know, O my God, what you would do to the *very little one* who answered your call, I continued my search and this is what I discovered: *"As one whom a mother caresses, so will I comfort you; you shall be carried at the breasts, and upon the knees they shall caress you.*

...The elevator which must raise me to heaven is Your arms, O Jesus! And for this I had no need to grow up, but rather I had to remain little...[56]

Once again we encounter her desire "to remain little," yet Thérèse did not consider her own point of view *insignificant:* she did not hesitate to instruct her own Prioress. Thérèse knew with certainty that hers was not a trivial life, that the emptying of all signs of human greatness had led her to the

---

[56]C, pp. 207, 8.

deep life she craved. Of the Christmas Eve when she regained her childhood "strength of soul" she wrote,

"Since that night I have never been defeated in any combat, but rather walked from victory to victory, beginning, so to speak, *'to run as a giant!'*"[57]

The linking of small and grand imagery is much in evidence toward the end of her life. In September of 1896 Thérèse had a persistent cough and dry throat. Realizing her youngest sister was quite ill Marie asked her to write down her "little doctrine."[58] In her long and passionate reply to Marie's question the spirit of littleness mingles with that strange boldness with God which also grew in Thérèse. She quoted Eliseus' prayer to Elias asking for HIS DOUBLE SPIRIT and then asked the inhabitants of heaven "to obtain for me YOUR TWOFOLD SPIRIT:"

> Jesus, I cannot fathom the depths of my request; I would be afraid to find myself overwhelmed under the weight of my bold desires. My excuse is that I am a *child,* and children do not reflect on the meaning of their words; however, their parents...do not hesitate to satisfy the desires of the *little ones* whom they love as much as they love themselves. To please them they do foolish things, even going to the extent of *becoming weak* for them...[59]

Living so closely with the other sisters, a few of whom had harsh personalities, a few of whom were neurotic, Thérèse saw greater need for small acts of love than for instruments of penance. But she did not substitute for the preoccupation with perfection and grand deeds a preoccupation with small deeds. The counterpoint to the pursuit of heroic deeds was not the pursuit of small deeds but a shift away from *any* accomplishment, however small, to an inner attitude of "remaining little," a consciousness that God upheld her "from instant to instant."

[57]A, p. 97.
[58]CL, p. 283.
[59]B. p. 196.

VI

Prayer

"Confiteor Deo omnipotenti, beatae Mariae semper Virgini, beato Michaeli Archangelo, beato Joanni Baptistae, sanctis Apostolis Petro et Paulo, omnibus Sanctis, et tibi, Pater, quia peccavi nimis cogitatione, verbo, et opera, mea culpa, mea culpa, mea maxima culpa..." [1]
The Confiteor—Ordinary of the Mass

"O Jesus...it seems to me that you cannot fill a soul with more love than the love with which you have filled mine;...I dare to ask you *'to love those whom you have given me with the love with which you loved me.'*"[2]
Thérèse, 1897

To glimpse the inner life of prayer of St. Thérèse in clear relief we must glance briefly at the tradition, the habits of prayer in which she was trained. One characteristic of the central prayer in the life of the Martin family, the Mass,

---

[1] I confess to Almighty God, to Blessed Mary, ever Virgin, to Blessed Michael the Archangel, to Blessed John the Baptist, to the Holy Apostles Peter and Paul, and to all the Saints, and to you, Father, that I have sinned exceedingly in thought, word and deed, through my fault, through my fault, through my most grievous fault...

[2] C, p. 256.

suggests the way the faithful approached God: it was said always in Latin. The language conveyed mystery, for the words were not all understood. Louis Martin's own effort to become a monk failed because he did not know Latin.[3] Despite the unknown words, the impact on the congregation was not the same as listening to a totally unfamiliar foreign tongue. Quite the opposite. The daily repetition of the same phrases, the yearly singing of the same ceremonial hymns, mingled the familiar with the mysterious.   For 7 hundred years the deaths of the faithful, priest or peasant, were mourned with the same chant:

Dies irae, dies illa
Solvet saeclum in favilla,
Teste David in Sibylla.

Quantus tremor est futurus,
Quando judex est venturus,
Cuncta stricte discussurus![4]

Heavy with old meaning, immune to the translator's fancy, this chanted poetry fixed over lifetimes recalled the unchanging quality of God and of the Catholic Faith.

For Zélie and Louis Martin's children the seasons of the year, the hours of the day were linked as well with prayers in French. Thérèse was taught to pray in the manner of the time among Catholic families—vocal prayers were the rule. In a decorated notebook which Pauline sent home two months before her 11 year old sister's first Communion,

[3]Guy Gaucher, *Histoire d'une Vie,* (Paris, Cerf, 1982), p. 8.

[4]Day of Wrath, thy fiery morning
Earth consumes,no longer scorning
David's and the Sibyl's warning.

Then what terror of each nation
When the Judge shall take his station
Strictly trying his creation!

The poem has 18 stanzas. It is a plea for mercy on the day of Judgment, written in the 13th century, and if we can judge from a statement of Bartholomew of Pisa, used in the liturgy of the dead from the year 1285. See Samuel Willoughby Duffield, *The Latin Hymn-Writers and Their Hymns* (New York, 1889), p. 247. Translation, p. 253.

Thérèse recorded clear examples of how Pauline taught her
to pray. She logged the number of times she repeated "invocations," brief phrases. By the day before her first Communion Thérèse had recorded 2,773 invocations, including,

"Little Jesus, I love you" (fifty times)

"Little Jesus, don't let me be proud anymore" (thirty
times)

"Little Jesus, may I always be simple and docile" (thirty-
five times)

"My whole heart is yours, Jesus" (thirty times)

"Little Jesus, I kiss you" (fifty times)[5]

Commonly people prayed *for* something: a favor, a cure;
sometimes they asked for signs. At age 14 Thérèse carried
out her famous test of praying for a favor. She fastened the
ideal of praying for "sinners" to the soul of the murderer
Henri Pranzini. As newspapers fed the French public's appetite for brutal details, Thérèse prayed. Though she stressed
that she would believe Pranzini saved without a sign, she
craved a sign, she asked for a sign. On the scaffold just
before he died Pranzini kissed the crucifix. Thérèse believed
her prayers were answered.[6]

Requests dominated her prayer on the day of profession,
the day when the Carmelites believed God listened carefully
to the prayer of a woman giving him her life. "Obliged" by
her sisters, she prayed for her father's cure.[7] And she prayed
for peace, and Jesus' love, and martyrdom and to be "forgotten like your little grain of sand" and "to save very many
souls."[8]

A dramatic appeal linked to a sign was rare in her life.
Convinced that God would give her anything she asked,
Thérèse became cautious about what she asked. The last
significant request for a favor for herself and a sign occurred
three years before her death. After Communion one day in

[5]GC, p. 191, ft. 4.

[6]A, p. 100.

[7]GCI, p. 644.

[8]SS, p. 275.

the Carmelite chapel Thérèse prayed for a sign that her father went "straight to heaven." The sign? That Sister Aimée of Jesus (a nun disgruntled by too many Martin sisters in her community) would drop her opposition to Céline's entering the Carmel. As Thérèse left chapel Sister Aimée told her she would no longer block Céline.[9] That was the final scene of a form of prayer that Thérèse now abandoned, not because her prayers were not answered, but because they *were*. All such particular desires were her own, not the will of God, even her prayer for martyrdom on the day of her profession. After Céline joined the Carmel Thérèse wrote:

"And now I have no other desire except *to love* Jesus unto folly. My childish desires have all flown away..."[10]

In the timing of this realization lies a startling irony, for Thérèse ceased to pray for specific favors for herself just at the time that the first symptoms of her own tuberculosis were appearing. Believing without question that God would grant her anything she asked, she continued to think any human want was simply her own "childish desire." Never did she pray for a cure; never did she pray even for an end to the pain.

*   *   *   *   *

At about age 11 Thérèse stumbled upon a deeper form of prayer.

"At this time in my life nobody had ever taught me how to make mental prayer, and yet I had a great desire to make it. Marie...allowed me to make only my vocal prayers."[11] Mental prayer. By this phrase Thérèse does not mean the practice of a learned method of praying. She had no free access to books. Her own description at age 22 of how she prayed about age 11 is distinctly not a formula.

[9] A, pp. 177-8.

[10] A, p. 178.

[11] A, p. 74.

One day, one of my teachers at the Abbey asked me what I did on my free afternoons when I was alone. I told her I went behind my bed in an empty space...and that it was easy to close myself in with my bed-curtain and that *"I thought."* "But what do you think about?" she asked. "I think about God, about life, about ETERNITY...I *think!"* The good religious laughed heartily at me, and later on she loved reminding me of the time when I *thought,* asking me if I *was still thinking.* I understand now that I was making mental prayer without knowing it and that God was already instructing me in secret.[12]

That the "good religious" laughed heartily suggests that she missed completely a major progression in Saint Thérèse's life: a step beyond conventional forms of prayer. Her sister Marie, also, failed to understand. She testified later that Thérèse asked her permission to make half an hour's prayer every day. Marie refused; she refused even a quarter of an hour. After Thérèse's death, in retrospect Marie explained that it frightened her—Thérèse was so devout.[13] Perhaps. But the conditions of Thérèse's discovery of another way to speak with God are foreign to the conventional notions of "devout." Thérèse describes yet another incident that occurred when she was 9, just after her jarring loss of her favorite sister Pauline to the Carmelites:

"The morning of the day I was to visit (Pauline), I was thinking things over in my *bed* (for it was there I made my profound meditations, and, contrary to the bride in the Canticles, I always found my Beloved there)..."[14] As often is the case in Thérèse's own writing (rarely in those who write about her) she plays with words—"profound meditations" is used lightly. Of importance here is that she considered herself to be praying while lying in her bed or wrapped up on the floor behind her bed, "thinking."

[12]A, pp.74-75.
[13]TE, p. 96.
[14]A, p. 71.

And she prayed in her attic room, the room in which she mingled memories of Pauline with live birds and flowers and a statue and cross. "It was in this room I loved to stay alone for hours on end to study and meditate before the beautiful view which stretched out before my eyes."[15] Her bedroom, her attic room served as sites of Thérèse's learning to think about God and to pray in a manner distinct from what those in charge of her had taught her.

Within the Carmel Thérèse developed another way to pray, distinct not only from the common manner of reciting fixed prayers and praying *for* something, but also from the common understanding of contemplative prayer among the nuns in the Carmel of Lisieux. They were Carmelites, wedded to their understanding of the contemplative ideal as molded by the great mystic St. Teresa of Avila.

* * * * *

The *Constitutions of the Religious Discalced Carmelites of the Primitive Observance* written by Teresa of Avila 300 years before Thérèse is a litany of detailed regulation. There are chapters on labor of the hands, silence and retreating to the cell, humility and penance, the sick, those who transgress, obedience and election of the superiors. The chapter entitled Canonical Hours and Spiritual Things stresses a quarter of an hour for examining the conscience after nine in the morning. Chanting is not only recommended, but regulated.

"The chant will never be in a tune, but intoned, in uniform voice..."[16] "For Grace after dinner, the nuns proceed at all times to the choir with the psalm *Miserere*..."[17] Certain psalms were sung traditionally at certain times: for the ceremony called The Chapter, psalms 66, 122, 129, which

[15]A, p. 91.

[16]*Regle Primitive et Constitutions des Religieuses de L'Ordre de Notre-Dame du Mont-Carmel selon La Reformation de Sainte Thérèse Pour Les Monastères de Son Ordre en France.* (Poitiers, Typographie de Henri Oudin, 1865), p. 52.

[17]*Ibid* p. 53.

were printed in the *Constitutions* in Latin. The *Rule*, the *Constitutions* governed every hour of the day, every activity including eating and speaking. Without permission, no nun could enter another's cell.

To focus on the *Constitutions* and the Primitive *Rule* (observed by the monks who withdrew to Mt. Carmel in the 12th century and reintroduced by St. Teresa of Avila) as the substance of the Carmelite life is misleading: they were the roadmap to another life. St. Teresa of Avila's reform aimed to shape the necessary externals of life to permit an interior life of prayer. Thus the emphasis on silence, on the Mass, the Divine Office, and meditation. Behind this strictly ordered life lay a history of belief that false activity entraps the human spirit, and that unfettered, the human will finds, not freedom, but a mask. A belief that the true self can be found only in union with God. The Rule disciplined the will.

Though an ideal of contemplative union existed in the Order in the person of St. Teresa of Avila, though each nun meditated on God as revealed through his creation, as revealed through his Word, Jesus, in practice it was presumptuous to think oneself the equal of St. Teresa of Avila.[18] She was called a mystic and known to have had visions, ecstasies. Ordinary nuns did not expect, nor did they seek, such a gift.

The Order cultivated an inner life of prayer with practical aids: the annual period of retreat, spiritual reading during meals (the lives of saints and the French translation of the Bible passages read in Latin in the Chapel that day), the recitation of commonly loved prayers such as the rosary, and many nuns had a spiritual advisor. Meditation was practiced daily, often by picturing a scene in the life of the Lord, pondering it, exploring the imagined details.

Thérèse obeyed the Carmelite *Rule* to the letter; but as with all received ideas, she put to the test the notions of prayer, and diverged from the strictly patterned route. If another nun's need conflicted with Thérèse's scheduled

[18]See GCI, p. 623, ft. 8.

prayer the human need won out. Though the period of silent evening prayer was vital to Thérèse, early in her novitiate she volunteered to help Sr. St. Pierre, the legendary crippled and irritable nun, from chapel to the dining room. At ten to six when Sr. St. Pierre shook her hour glass Thérèse abruptly stopped her own evening prayer.[19]

Thérèse's periods of retreat—days of prayer intended to be the time of refreshment and renewal—were generally dry.

"Ask Jesus to make me generous during my retreat," she wrote to Pauline just before the ceremony in which she received the Carmelite habit. "He is riddling me with *pinpricks;* the poor little ball is exhausted. All over it has very little holes which make it suffer more than if it had only one large one!...Nothing near Jesus. Aridity!.."[20] For three years Thérèse voluntarily made her annual retreats with Sister Martha of Jesus,[21] a neurotic nun who sometimes directed her anger at Thérèse. During these retreats Thérèse accepted Sister Martha's method of keeping a tally of individual "sacrifices" and "acts of virtue" similar to what Pauline taught her when she was 11.[22] Retreats, then, were not the source of her renewed prayer life.

According to Céline, Thérèse cautioned the novices she advised against relying on a Spiritual Director.

"More often than not," she told the novices, "you will find Jesus only after you have left all creatures behind."[23]

The many formal prayers commonly recited from holy cards or prayer books?

"Outside the *Divine Office* which I am very unworthy to recite," she wrote Mother Marie de Gonzague at the end of her life, "I do not have the courage to force myself to search out *beautiful* prayers in books. There are so many of them it

[19]C, p. 247.

[20]Thérèse to Pauline, LT 74, Jan. 6, 1889, GCI, p. 499.

[21]Though older than Thérèse and professed in the same month, Sister Martha of Jesus requested permission to remain in the Novitiate with Thérèse. TE, p. 216.

[22]TE, p. 217.

[23]TE, p. 134.

really gives me a headache! and each prayer is more *beautiful* than the others..."[24] But she loved the prayers said together with the community.

"I feel then that the fervor of my sisters makes up for my lack of fervor; but when alone (I am ashamed to admit it) the recitation of the rosary is more difficult for me than the wearing of an instrument of penance...I force myself in vain to meditate on the mysteries of the rosary; I don't succeed in fixing my mind on them..."[25] When she felt so arid that it was "impossible to draw forth one single thought to unite me with God, I *very slowly* recite an "Our Father..."[26] Though no more conscious of what was occurring than she had been conscious of praying in the old days when she sat behind her bed and thought about God, Thérèse's difficulty with conventional forms signaled, according to the teaching of John of the Cross, the call to contemplation.

* * * * *

Within Thérèse existed two major obstacles to the deeper life she sought: self-torment and her own self-centered will. She recognized both and began to fight them before entering the Carmel. Nearly all of her life Thérèse battled to break her own will; she fought the attachment to her own whims, her own emotions. The instruments of penance, the individual sacrifices, the pursuit of perfection within the Carmel failed to attract her as did her one overriding goal of breaking her own will. Since the lengths to which she went are detailed in Chapter II they need not be repeated here, except to stress that detachment from everything that was not God— including her own feelings—was for her the vital precondition of a deepening inner life. The other obstacle, self-torment, appears at first glance the opposite of a self-centered will. But as Thérèse recognized, it was related: in each case one's own emotional reactions blot out all else. Each effec-

[24]C, p. 242.
[25]*Ibid.*
[26]C, p. 243.

tively eclipses one's inner silence. Her battle against self-torment is focused, intense, and clear. It began at an identifiable time.

"It was during my retreat for the second Communion (age 12) that I was assailed by the terrible sickness of scruples. One would have to pass through this martyrdom to understand it well, and for me to express what I suffered for *a year and a half* would be impossible. All my most simple thoughts and actions became the cause of trouble for me..."[27] "Scruples" was the irrational terror of having committed a deadly sin. This terror led to dissecting simple actions and thoughts over and over again to determine if one had consented to sins, especially consented to "impurity." The label "scruples" suggests an overreaction, the distortion by an oversensitive mind of what was taught to it, a fault in the listener. In fact, the manner in which priests still infected with a Jansenist sense of evil taught religion to the impressionable young served as a catalyst. Among otherwise normal Catholic girls, scruples were not uncommon.[28]

Thérèse's early childhood revealed no such torment.[29] She enjoyed her first confession.

"...I made my confession like a *big girl* and received his blessing with *great devotion*...Coming out of the confessional I was so happy and light-hearted that I had never felt so much joy in my soul..."[30] Her training came from Pauline who "urged her to sentiments of love and gratitude rather

---

[27]A, p. 84.

[28]Among the seven girls in the Martin and Guérin family, two others besides Thérèse (that we know of) were tormented by scruples: her sister Marie, and her cousin Marie Guérin. Each case developed independently at different times—her sister Marie's torment was earlier, without Thérèse's being aware of it. Marie Guérin's difficulties were later.

[29]Following the hysterical illness when Thérèse was age 10, she felt she had lied about the statue coming alive and smiling at her. She also had doubts about the reality of her illness. For a time, she said, "I was unable to look upon myself without a feeling of *profound horror*." This might be interpreted as a period of guilt akin to that launched by the Abbè Domin's sermon. See A, p. 67.

[30]A, pp. 40-41.

than to contrition."[31] Her retreat for her first Communion, and the first Communion itself indicated a child who drew joy from her religious life. She was "assailed by the terrible sickness of scruples" as the direct result of a sermon by the school chaplain during the retreat for her second Communion when she was 12. The sermon the Abbè Domin preached on mortal sin shattered Thérèse's peace. Her retreat notes, quoted earlier, merit a second look:

"What the abbè told us was frightening. He spoke about mortal sin, and he described a soul in the state of sin and how much God hated it. He compared it to a little dove soaked in mud, and who is no longer able to fly."[32] For a year and a half fear that natural reactions and common thoughts were mortally sinful, fear that she might be committing sacrilege paralyzed Thérèse emotionally. With strict and consistent rules against Thérèse confessing these fears as "sins," Marie gradually loosened this vise of terror.

In a remarkable letter written at age 16 to her cousin Marie Guérin, Thérèse appears not only to be free of this torment, but to view it clearly as distortion. Her cousin Marie Guérin, then nearly 19 and visiting Paris, wrote Thérèse at the Carmel. The letter, and Thérèse's reply, convey both the crippling power of this fear and the firm judgment and self-discipline with which Thérèse fought off the notion that inner torment is a part of religion. Marie Guérin's letter:

> My dear Thérèse,
> . . . I know in advance that you are not going to be pleased with me, but what do you expect, I am suffering so much that it does me good to pour all my pains into your heart. Paris was not made for healing the scrupulous; I no longer know where to turn my eyes. If I flee from one nudity, I meet another, and so it goes on all day long. It's enough to make you die of sorrow; it seems to me I do this out of curiosity, I have to be looking everywhere. It

---

[31]TE, p. 38.

[32]Six, *La Veritable Enfance de Thérèse de Lisieux,* p. 201. (Thérèse's retreat notes, quoted from P. Francois de Sainte-Marie: *Notes et Tables,* pp. 22-27.)

seems to do that is to see evil. I don't know if you will
understand me; I have so much in my poor head that I
don't know how to sort it out. Neither does the demon fail
to bring to my mind all these evil things that I saw during
the day, and this is another subject of torment. How do
you expect me to receive Holy Communion tomorrow
and Friday?...[33]

Thérèse wrote a letter in return that aimed to wipe away
Marie's self-torture as her sister Marie had wiped away her
own:

> You did well to write me, and I understand *everything*
> ...*everything, everything, everything*...!
> You haven't committed the *shadow of any evil;* I can
> assure you of this without any fear, and, besides, Jesus
> tells me this in the depths of my heart... We must despise all
> these temptations and pay no attention whatsoever to
> them.

Urging her cousin to receive Communion, Thérèse continues:

> ... I hear you saying to me: 'Thérèse is saying this because
> she doesn't know I really do it on purpose...it pleases
> me...and so I cannot receive Communion since I believe
> I would commit a sacrilege...' Yes, your poor little Thé-
> rèse does know; I tell you that she understands it
> *all*...She, too, has passed through the *martyrdom* of
> scruples, but Jesus has given her the grace to receive
> Communion just the same, even when she believed that
> she had committed *great sins*...[34]

At age 16 Thérèse appeared to be free of the self-torment
of scruples. With its code of rules and vigilance against
faults, however, the Carmel's atmosphere could entrap a
sensitive idealistic young girl who had fastened her dreams
on living solely for God. "Imperfections," "faults" were

---

[33]Marie Guérin to Thérèse, IC 113, May 29, 1889, GCI, pp. 565-6.
[34]Thérèse to Marie Guérin, IT 92, May 30, 1889, GCI, p. 567-8.

committed daily. Not until she made her retreat at age 18 with Father Alexis Prou was Thérèse finally freed from anxiety about ordinary reactions such as feeling tired during prayer. Father Prou decisively cleared the path for a new level of prayer when he swept away Thérèse's anxiety: "...Never had I heard that our faults *could not cause God any pain,* and this assurance filled me with joy...My nature was such that fear made me recoil; with *love* not only did I advance, I actually *flew.*"[35] The inner calm that came in the wake of being freed from worry about the state of her soul was absolutely essential to Thérèse's life of prayer. This freedom altered her view of what God saw in her. Even her irritations with the other sisters, her falling asleep during Mass, her "arid" prayer life, ceased to bother her. After her conference with Father Prou *no* failure of her own contained any power to torment her.

"Really, I am far from being a saint," she wrote two years before she died, "and...instead of rejoicing, for example, at my aridity, I should attribute it to my little fervor and lack of fidelity; I should be desolate for having slept (for seven years) during my hours of prayer and my *thanksgivings* after Holy Communion; well, I am not desolate. I remember that *little children* are as pleasing to their parents when they are asleep as well as when they are wide awake...I remember, too, that when they perform operations, doctors put their patients to sleep."[36] As John of the Cross stressed, *any* inner turbulence, *any* anxiety, *any* form of absorption in one's self was an enemy. In Thérèse's case this meant torment over the state of her own soul. Thérèse was convinced of the teaching of John of the Cross; for God to be all, she must be nothing.[37]

* * * * *

The tone of the formal prayer life familiar to Thérèse can be seen in this example of commonly recited prayers:

[35]A, p. 174.

[36]A, p. 165.

[37]For example: LA, p. 137, no . 4; LA, p. 141, No. 1.

We beseech you, O Lord, in your clemency, be pleased to govern your Church which you have nourished with the sacred repast, so that, guided by your mighty rule, she may enjoy greater freedom and continue in the fullness of her faith. Through Our Lord, Jesus Christ, your Son, who lives and reigns with you in the unity of the Holy Spirit, God, world without end. Amen.[38]

By contrast, the following is an example of Thérèse's prayer toward the end of her life:

Jesus, O Jesus, if the *desire* of *loving You* is so delightful, what will it be to possess and enjoy this Love?

How can a soul as imperfect as mine aspire to the possession of the plenitude of *Love?* O Jesus, my first and only Friend, You whom I love *UNIQUELY, explain this mystery to me! Why do You not reserve these great aspirations for great souls, for the* Eagles *that soar in the heights?*[39]

Thérèse's letter to her sister Marie which contained these and other intimate words that surge in a cry of love opens with a caution: "Do not believe I am swimming in consolations; oh, no, my consolation is to have none on earth."[40] Contradiction? Not according to St. John of the Cross, for whom the desire for "consolation" in prayer was itself a desire not for God but for a human emotion. Thérèse's difficulty with normal methods of prayer was a sign of the true contemplative pointed out explicitly by John of the Cross.

By the end of her life Thérèse disliked all spiritual reading except the Gospels; she disliked, too, prayers polished with abstract words. She did not "meditate." Picturing scenes, pondering ideas meant drawing from her own imagination. Thérèse distrusted her own imagination. Her creative power lay in *perception*, in connecting the words of particular pas-

[38] Postcommunion prayer of the Common of One or More Supreme Pontiffs. *St. Joseph Daily Missal* (Catholic Book Publishing Co., New York, 1959), p. 1153.

[39] B, p. 197.

[40] B, p. 187.

sages from scripture with her own very concrete perceptions of her life.

"...for a long time you permitted me to be bold with You. You have said to me as the father of the prodigal son said to his older son: '*EVERYTHING that is mine is yours.*' Your words, O Jesus, are mine, then, and I can make use of them to draw upon the souls united to me the favors of the heavenly Father."[41] This leap in Thérèse's life of prayer does not depend on imagined scenes any more than on the practical aids of the Carmel. Thérèse had entered a state of prayer that left behind scenes, reading, meditating, whether on ideas or images, left behind all techniques of prayer.

> O Jesus, Your *little bird* is happy to be *weak and little.* What would become of it if it were big? Never would it have the boldness to appear in Your presence, *to fall asleep* in front of You...[42]

What did prayer mean to Thérèse? The summer that she died she explained to her Prioress:

"For me, *prayer* is an aspiration of the heart, it is a simple glance directed to heaven, it is a cry of gratitude and love in the midst of trial as well as joy; finally, it is something great, supernatural, which expands my soul and unites me to Jesus."[43] Thérèse went further than such simple, direct expressions of her sentiments to Jesus. She addressed the Father intimately too. That God was his *Father*, not a remote deity who gloried in animal sacrifices, lay at the core of Jesus' message. Yet nearly 1900 years after his death, with the exception of the Lord's Prayer it was customary to approach God less as Father than as The Almighty.

"Grant, we beseech you, Almighty God..." Learning from Jesus, Thérèse addressed him personally, as a Father. In this prayer she borrowed Jesus' own words (according to St. John) in speaking to his Father the night before he died:

---

[41]C, pp. 255-6.
[42]B, p. 199.
[43]C, p. 242.

"I pray for them, not for the world do I pray, but for those whom you have given me, because they are yours; and all things that are mine are yours, and yours are mine...
Father, I will that where I am, these also whom you have given me may be with me..."
Yes, Lord, this is what I would like to repeat after You before flying into Your arms. Perhaps this is boldness? No, for a long time You permitted me to be bold with You...[44]

She speaks to the Father as intimately as Jesus did. As René Laurentin points out, Thérèse is no longer prostrate in unworthiness before a remote deity. She "embraced the crucifix not by the feet but by the face."[45] When speaking to Jesus, when speaking to the Father, Thérèse has risen from her knees.

A mystic? Thérèse never applied the term to herself. It suggests to those innocent of the inner life unfamiliar, imagined experiences. As we have seen, Thérèse cautioned her sisters repeatedly during the last summer against their assumptions about her inner life.[46]

* * * * *

Union with God on earth was the highest ideal of a Carmelite. But most of the nuns in the little monastery of Lisieux would have been quite surprised at the suggestion that Sister Thérèse of the Child Jesus knew contemplative union with God. Sister Thérèse was clearly not a grand personage renowned in the Church for heroic deeds, not even for the slightest status in monastic life. She had no status. The basis of her life of prayer would have surprised them still more. She said clearly that her inner life of prayer did not depend on the tradition of perfection pursued by the Carme-

---

[44]C, p. 255.

[45]René Laurentin, *Thérèse de Lisieux, Mythes et Réalité* (Paris, 1972), p. 139.

[46]With regard to mystical experience, see Chapter III.

lites.[47] It was not hers by virtue of having shut out the world
to live the ascetic life of the Carmelite. Her intimacy with
God rested, she said, on her "littleness."[48] Thérèse's moving
letter to her sister Marie in 1896, in which she forgets herself
in a written prayer to Jesus, ends with this plea:

> O Jesus! why can't I tell all *little souls* how unspeakable is
> Your condescension? I feel that if You found a soul
> weaker and littler than mine... You would be pleased to
> grant it still greater favors, provided it abandoned itself
> with total confidence in Your Infinite Mercy. But why do I
> desire to communicate Your secrets of Love, O, Jesus, for
> was it not You alone who taught them to me, and can
> You not reveal them to others? Yes, I know it, and I beg
> You to do it. I beg You to cast Your Divine Glance upon
> a great number of *little* souls. I beg You to choose a legion
> of *little* Victims worthy of Your Love![49]

The notion conveyed by the Latin prayers of a God as fixed
as the language itself suggested a static quality. One "said" or
"recited" prayers as one tried to imagine The Lord as he
lived hundreds of years earlier. But Thérèse believed that
Jesus and the Father were listening to her at the moment she
was speaking, that what she said mattered as it would in any
changing human relationship. Not linked to any emotional
state either of ecstasy or of "recollection," Thérèse's prayer
was a spontaneous conversation whether she were happy,
sad, or sleepy. The fixed ideal in the minds of the faithful of
contemplative union was a human construct as much as the
attachment to an idea, to a whim, to the "beautiful" prayers
in books.

And once again Thérèse diverges from the commonly held
view of her time. This life of prayer was not restricted to a

[47]For example, LA, p. 137, No. 4.
[48]B, p. 200.
[49]*Ibid.*

very few great souls; it was not "presumptuous" to seek it. If this warm, spontaneous, personal life of prayer could be *hers,* it was not limited to great saints and monastics who climb the ladder of perfection. For a legion of souls to know her intimacy with Jesus, with the Father, depended on their littleness, and his "Divine Glance."

VII

Thérèse, The Priesthood, and Priests

> "...let us save especially the souls of priests; these souls should be more transparent than crystal...how many bad priests, priests who are not holy enough...Let us pray, let us suffer for them..."[1]
> Thérèse (age 16) to Céline, 1889

> "You see, God is going to take me at an age when I would not have had the time to become a priest...If I could have been a priest, I would have been ordained at these June ordinations..."[2]
> Thérèse (age 24), 1897

Thérèse's pilgrimage to Rome before entering the Carmel yielded a crucial insight: the sacred functions of the priesthood were exercised by ordinary men. Until Canon Delatroëtte blocked her from entering the Carmel of Lisieux Thérèse had not thought that a priest might be wrong. And until the trip to Rome she had not thought that a priest's soul might not be pure.

---

[1]Thérèse to Céline, LT 94, July 14, 1889, GCI, p. 578.
[2]TE, p. 155.

But on the pilgrimage the priests who morning after morning consecrated the Sacred Host dined night after night elegantly with the nobility. Father Révérony, the bishop's assistant, shared his carriage only with nobles of high rank, and then only the men. Left behind by accident one day in Assisi, Thérèse had to ride with Father Révérony and the gentlemen.

"Before we reached the station, all the *great personages* took their huge purses out to give some money to the driver (already paid). I did the same thing, taking out my *very* little purse. Father Révérony did not agree with what I drew out from it, some pretty *little* coins, and instead he offered a *large* coin for both of us."[3]

At age 14 Thérèse decided to dedicate her life in the Carmel to praying for the souls of priests.

"I understood *my vocation* in Italy," she wrote 8 years later, "and that's not going too far in search of such useful knowledge. I lived in the company of many *saintly priests* for a month and I learned that, though their dignity raises them above the angels, they are nevertheless weak and fragile men."[4]

As usual in Thérèse's life this lesson drawn from experience held. Prior to her final profession when questioned formally about her intentions she answered, "I came to save souls, especially to pray for priests."[5]

* * * * *

As a small child Thérèse knew priests only from the distance of their official functions: on the altar, teaching the catechism in class, behind the confessional grille. The summer after Pauline left home the ten year old Thérèse met Father Almiré Pichon, who served as an advisor to her sister Marie and was becoming a friend of the family. A woman pursuing a life of the spirit customarily chose a priest to

[3]A, p. 139.
[4]A, p. 122.
[5]A, p. 149.

serve as her spiritual director. The next May Thérèse wrote to tell Father Pichon "that soon I would be a Carmelite and then he would be my director..."[6] But by the time she entered the Carmel Thérèse had made another discovery: she needed no spiritual director. In her copybook of memories she wrote about herself at age 14:

> ...I went to confession only a few times, and never spoke about my interior sentiments. The way I was walking was so straight, so clear, I needed no other guide but Jesus. I compared directors to faithful mirrors, reflecting Jesus in souls, and I said that for me God was using no intermediary, he was acting directly![7]

Thérèse distinguished sharply between acceptance of the priest's sacramental authority and opening her "interior sentiments" to the priest's gaze and advice. In the same passage Thérèse wrote that her confessor permitted her to receive Communion four times a week during the month of May. Yet she so strictly guarded her own inner life that her confessor learned about his young penitent's efforts to gain entry to the Lisieux Carmel from the newspaper. While Thérèse was in Rome an article appeared referring to "a young girl of fifteen, who begged the Holy Father for permission to enter a convent immediately..." The Pope's counsel that she be patient and pray "caused the young girl to break down into sobs."[8] After reading the article her baffled confessor appeared at the Carmel speakroom and heard of Thérèse's plan from Marie Martin.[9]

Thérèse's reluctance to disclose her inner life continued within the Carmel. The month after she entered, discouraged by her continuous "faults," and "imperfections," Thérèse tried to explain her struggle to Father Pichon, the director she chose at age 11:

[6]GC I, introductory note, p. 376.
[7]A, p. 105.
[8]GCI, pp. 376., introductory note.
[9]Pauline to Isidore Guérin, LD, Nov. 28-9, 1887, GCI, p. 376.

"My interview with the good Father was a great consolation to me, but it was veiled in tears because I experienced much difficulty in confiding in him."[10] Father Pichon performed one important service for Thérèse: he declared solemnly that she had never committed a mortal sin.[11] Within a year he had settled in Canada. Though Thérèse wrote him regularly for the rest of her life, according to Pauline "he wrote her a few lines once a year."[12] He was a kind man but blind to Thérèse's depth. His letters contain affectionate phrases and encouraging words and advice general enough to be meant for anyone; they reveal no particular insight into Thérèse.

Pauline has testified that in Thérèse's early years in the Carmel "fear of offending God was poisoning her life."[13] Father Pichon wrote to Thérèse five months after her Profession, during this period of struggle. The tone is characteristic of his letters:

"... Were you not well pampered to receive the blessing of the Holy Father?...oh! pampered in all ways? I was quite touched by seeing your crown of white roses blessed by the venerated Patriarch, and posed on the white hair..."[14] A measure of Father Pichon's failure to perceive Thérèse accurately is that he saved none of her letters, not even a major letter written two months before she died about which Thérèse said "...it was my whole soul."[15] That last summer Thérèse told Pauline: "Father Pichon treated me too much like a child."[16]

Slowly, alone, Thérèse was carving out a distinctive sanctity which met with many obstacles not the least of which was finding a priest who understood her. During her early

[10]A, p. 149.

[11]*Ibid.*

[12]TE, p. 52.

[13]TE, p. 66.

[14]Père Pichon to Thérèse, LC 146, Feb. 16, 1891, CGII, p. 632.

[15]CG II, p. 1056, ft. a.

[16]LA, p. 73.

days in the Carmel Thérèse confessed to the chaplain, Father Youf, that she had trouble staying awake during Mass. According to Pauline, "he gave her a severe reprimand and told her that she was offending God."[17] A sickly man, Father Youf disliked being asked for spiritual counsel outside the confessional.[18] But even if he had offered counsel, he was ill-equipped to help Thérèse. Toward the end of her life Thérèse confided to him her doubts about an afterlife. Pauline testified that Thérèse's doubts frightened Father Youf. He warned her not to dwell on them; they were dangerous.[19] To a visiting priest Thérèse confided her desire to be a great saint; he told her this was "sheer pride."[20]

During her retreat in 1891, three and a half years after she entered the Carmel, Thérèse finally met a priest who understood her. As we have seen, Father Alexis Prou recognized Thérèse's essential conflict clearly: she wanted to feel confident in her love of God, yet the fear of continuously failing him paralyzed her. Her problem lay not in her faults but in her fear. Father Prou simply told Thérèse her perceptions were right—she should go ahead with confidence for she could not hurt God.

"After speaking only a few words, I *was understood* in a marvelous way...."[21]

This session took place six years before Thérèse died. Having finally found a priest who could guide her Thérèse asked permission to see him again. Mother Marie de Gonzague refused.[22] In this single brief session in the confessional Father Prou became the last living priest to have a significant impact on Thérèse. In the critical years in which she

---

[17]GC I p. 659, ft. 5 (refers to NPPA, Prudence, Director).

[18]TE, p. 247.

[19]TE, p. 123.

[20]TE, p. 52.

[21]A, p. 173.

[22]TE, p. 212, and Piat, *St. Thérèse de Lisieux à la Découverte a la Voie d'Enfance,* (Paris, 1964), pp. 124-5.

searched out and found her own path to God Thérèse had no human spiritual director.

"Jesus," she wrote Marie the year before she died, "teaches me in secret."[23]

The year before she died Thérèse learned of Theóphane Vénard, a French missionary to Indochina publicly executed in Hanoi in 1861 at age 31. During her last year Théophane became Thérèse's ideal priest. He was young when he died, happily died a martyr's death, wrote cheerful letters to his family, had a light sense of humor, and was the missionary she could never be. During her final months alive she kept his picture tacked to her bed curtain.

Driven literally underground, Théophane had to breathe through holes in the ground. His letters, written from this hideout, convey a lilting quality and vivid details reminiscent of Thérèse's style. He lived, he said, like "a poor plant in a cellar," with spiders, rats and toads for companions, the only news being the daily reports of the torture of Christians. The reports rattled his nerves.

"I live on without being too bilious; my weakness is my nerves. I need something strengthening like wine, but we have barely enough to say Mass, so one must not think of it."[24]

When Théophane was captured he was chained by the neck and ankles in a bamboo cage and taken to Tonkin (Hanoi). After two months in his cage he wrote home:

"Can you picture me sitting quietly in the middle of my wooden cage, born by eight soldiers, beseiged on all sides by a huge crowd who almost barred the passage of the troops? 'What a pretty little fellow that European is!' I heard some of them saying. 'He is as gay and cheerful as if he were going to a feast. He doesn't look a bit afraid.'"[25]

Thirteen days after he wrote these words Théophane was paraded through the streets, removed from his cage and

---

[23]B, p. 187.

[24]Letter from Théophane Vénard, in Benedictine of Stanbrook Abbey, *Letters from the Saints*, (N.Y., 1964), p. 57.

[25]*Ibid*, p. 263.

executed publicly by means of a cruel, slow beheading. It was not his martyr's death which appealed so much to Thérèse but Théophane himself, a real human being brought alive through his letters. She was accustomed to lives of the saints being read aloud in the refectory, such as that of St. Louis de Gonzague. "Théophane Vénard pleases me much more than St. Louis de Gonzague," Thérèse told Pauline. "...the life of...(St. Louis) is extraordinary, and that of Théophane is very ordinary. Besides, he is the one who is talking, whereas for the Saint someone else is telling the story and making him speak; so we know practically nothing about his 'little' soul! Théophane Vénard loved his family very much...I don't understand the saints who don't love their family..." [26] A few months before she died Thérèse composed an "entirely personal" poem in Théophane's honor. An excerpt:

> ...Your brief exile was a sweet canticle
> Whose accents know how to touch hearts
> And for Jesus, your poet's soul
> At each instant made flowers spring to life
> Rising toward the celestial sphere
> Your chant of farewell was still full of spring
> You murmured: "Me, the little ephemeral one
> In the fair heavens, I am going to be first!"
>
> ...To suffer for God seemed to you a delight
> Smiling, you knew how to live and to die...[27]

* * * * *

[26]LA, pp. 46-7.

[27]*Poésies,* p. 217. The selection is the second and part of the third stanza of a seven stanza rhymed poem.

> Ton court exil fut comme un doux cantique
> Dont les accents savaient toucher les coeurs
> Et pour Jésus, ton âme poétique
> A chaque instant faisant nâitre des fleurs.
> En t'èlevant vers la Céleste sphère
> Ton chant d'adieu fut encor printanier
> <moi petit éphémère
> Dans le beau Ciel, je m'en vais le premier!...>
> ...Souffrir pour Dieu te semblait un délice.
> En souriant, tu sus vivre et mourir...

In the letter she wrote to her sister Marie in 1896 in which she described finding her vocation, Thérèse addressed these words to Jesus:

"I feel in me the *vocation of* the PRIEST. With what love, O Jesus, I would carry You in my hands when, at my voice, You would come down from heaven. And with what love would I give You to souls! But alas! while desiring to be a *Priest,* I admire and envy the humility of St. Francis of Assisi and I feel the *vocation* of imitating him in refusing the sublime dignity of the *Priesthood.* "[28]

In Thérèse's era there was no talk of women priests. The idea of a woman desiring the priesthood would have appeared absurd. When her bishop heard of the manuscript of Thérèse's childhood memories "his first reaction was one of distrust of the female imagination."[29] But Thérèse had seen worldy priests; she had sought direction and learned the difficulty of finding a priest who understood her; she had listened to sermons that terrified her and sermons that distorted the scriptures. These were flaws of the priests; to Thérèse, the priesthood itself was a sacred trust. She consciously wished she could have been a priest, and she discussed with her sisters what she would have done.[30]

She was eager to know the actual words used in the ancient scriptures and the literal words spoken by Jesus; differences in scriptural translation disturbed Thérèse.[31] Training in the ancient languages was not open to her, but had she been a priest, she told Céline, she would have studied Greek and Hebrew to know God's thought as he expressed it.[32] Sermons in which priests gave free reign to their own imaginations instead of striving for a clear, precise description based on scripture bothered her. Her sermons

[28] B, p. 192.

[29] TE, pp. 273, 4.

[30] Céline testified at the Process, "The sacrifice of not being able to be a priest was something she always felt deeply." TE, pp. 155-6.

[31] TE, p. 122.

[32] *Ibid.* pp. 122-3.

would not have relied on pious stories or imagined scenes with no basis in scripture.

"How I would have loved to be a priest in order to preach about the Blessed Virgin!" she told Pauline the summer she died.

> One sermon would be sufficient to say everything. . . I'd first make people understand how little is known by us about her life. . . at the age of three. . . (she) went up to the Temple to offer herself to God burning with sentiments of love and extraordinary fervor. While perhaps she went there very simply out of obedience to her parents. . .
>
> I must see her real life, not her imagined life. I'm sure that her real life was very simple. They show her to us as unapproachable but they should present her as imitable. . . she is more Mother than Queen. . . [33]

In June, 1897, Thérèse told Céline she would die that year before she would have "had the time to become a priest. If I could have been a priest, I would have been ordained at these June ordinations." [34]

*   *   *   *   *

On her Profession Day Thérèse prayed for a favor: ". . . not able to be a priest," she wrote of herself, "she wanted a priest to receive in her place the Lord's graces, to have the same aspirations, the same desires as she. . ." [35] Toward the end of her life Thérèse corresponded with two young men, one a missionary priest, the other an aspiring priest. Had her letters been stiff and formal the correspondence between Thérèse, a cloistered nun, and these two young men would nevertheless be unusual. But the warmth flowing through her letters and her interest in their lives make this correspondence extraordinary. These letters furnish the clearest examples of the manner in which Thérèse

[33]LA, p. 161.

[34]TE, p. 155.

[35]Thérèse to P. Roulland, LT 201, Nov. 1, 1896, CGII, p. 908.

guided souls under her care. Her interest was strong, consistent and pierced through the formal distance and vague pieties common in her day.

A dry cough and sore throat, harbingers of tuberculosis, already plagued Thérèse in October, 1895 when Pauline sought her out one day in the laundry room. As Prioress, she gave Thérèse a letter from a seminarian preparing for life as a missionary priest, asking for a spiritual sister to pray for his soul.[36]

"I would really have to go back to my childhood days to recapture once more the memory of joys so great that the soul is too little to contain them," Thérèse wrote later of her reaction. "...I felt my soul was renewed; it was as if someone had struck for the first time musical strings left forgotten..."[37] But military service distracted Maurice Bellière, both from Thérèse and the priesthood. She heard nothing from him until the following summer.[38]

The following May, Mother Marie de Gonzague, reelected Prioress, assigned Thérèse a second spiritual brother scheduled to be ordained within weeks and to leave for China that summer. Thérèse asked Adolphe Roulland to send her the significant dates in his life; one of them was September 8, 1890. Doubting his call to the priesthood, Roulland prayed that day in a Normandy shrine. While he prayed his doubts cleared; the decision was "suddenly and definitively fixed in my mind."[39] September 8, 1890 was the date of Thérèse's Profession, the day she asked Jesus to give a priest grace in her stead. Their "union" began, Thérèse told Adolphe Roulland, on that day six years earlier.[40]

"...my Brother," she addressed him soon after her sole

[36]C, p. 251.

[37]*Ibid.*

[38]Piat, *Thérèse de Lisieux à la Découverte de la Voie D'Enfance,*, p. 272. According to Father Piat, Maurice Bellière had the impression that he was not permitted to write directly to Thérèse.

[39]CL, p. 293, 4, ft. 60.

[40]Thérèse to P. Roulland, LT 201, Nov. 1896, CGII, p. 908.

meeting with him at the Carmel, "...distance can never separate our souls, even death will only make our union more intimate. If I go to Heaven soon, I shall ask Jesus' permission to visit you in Su-Chuen, and we shall continue our apostolate together. Meanwhile I shall always be united to you by prayer, and I ask our Lord never to let me be joyful when you are suffering..."[41]

Father Roulland did suffer in those early days in China, but not physical pain. China in the 1890's was an inhospitable place for foreigners; the Boxer Rebellion occurred at the close of the decade. Martyrdom was not so remote a possibility: within the year that Father Roulland arrived a French Catholic priest was murdered.[42]

"At this moment we are not in imminent danger of death," wrote Father Roulland from China,

> but from one day to the next, we might be stabbed; we should not be martyrs in the full sense of the term, but if we direct our intention aright—if we say, for instance, 'My God, it is for love of you that we have come here, accept the sacrifice of our lives and convert our souls'— should we not be martyrs enough to go to Heaven? ...One young man...(was) strangled and cooked in a pot; they offered this dish to the person who told us the story and saw the victim's two legs...if the brigands murder me and I am not worthy to enter immediately into Heaven, you will haul me out of Purgatory and I shall go and wait for you in Paradise.[43]

Despite his effort to make light of his fears Thérèse detected the priest's anxiety about the state of his soul. She focused on his distorted view. Father Roulland was bound by the common assumption that God's justice must be satisfied to the letter with punishment, with purging. Thé-

[41]Thérèse to P. Roulland, LT 193, July 30, 1896, CGII, p. 877.

[42]In April a priest ordained with Père Roulland was murdered. (Père Mazel). CL p. 330, ft. 54.

[43]P. Roulland to Thérèse LC 175, Feb. 24, 1897, CGII, pp. 954-5.

rèse rejected the idea of God as a harsh judge. In her next letter she bluntly told the young priest so, and summed up her view of God's justice:

> I do not understand, my brother, why you seem to doubt of your immediate entry into heaven, if the infidels took your life. I know one must be very pure to appear before the God of all Holiness, but I know too that the Lord is infinitely just; and it is this justice, which terrifies so many souls, that is the basis of my joy and trust. To be just means not only to exercise severity in punishing the guilty, but also to recognize right intentions and reward virtue. I hope as much from the good God's justice as from His mercy... For He knows our frailty. He remembers that we are only dust. As a father has tenderness for his children, so the Lord has compassion on us!... O my Brother ...how can we doubt that the good God will open the gates of His kingdom to His children who have loved Him to the point of sacrificing all for Him... How can He possibly let Himself be vanquished in generosity? How can He purify in the flames of purgatory souls consumed by the fire of divine love?... [44]

Not one missionary, she told him, should go to Purgatory. Thérèse did not hesitate to teach this priest *her* way.

> ... I don't understand souls who are afraid of so tender a Friend. Sometimes, when I read spiritual treatises, in which perfection is shown with a thousand obstacles in the way and encircled with a throng of illusions, my poor little mind grows very soon weary, I close the learned book which splits my head and parches my heart, and I take the Holy Scripture. Then all seems luminous, a single word opens up infinite horizons to my soul, perfection seems easy, I see that it is enough to realize one's nothingness, and to abandon oneself like a child into the arms of the good God.
>
> Leaving to great souls, great minds, the fine books I

[44]Thérèse to P. Roulland, LT 226, May 9, 1897, CGII, p. 983.

can't understand, still less put into practice, I rejoice to be
little because only children and those who are like them
will be admitted to the heavenly banquet...[45]

A week after she had been moved to the Carmel infirmary
to die Thérèse wrote to say goodbye to Father Roulland.
Her nights were plagued with fever and the day before she
wrote the letter she had suffered terrible pain in her side. Her
hands were emaciated.[46] Her reply to his letter in which he
had described learning Chinese displays no hint of the pain
she had been through, no hint of her exhaustion. She writes
playfully of the milk diet which caused her continual
vomiting:

> My Brother,
>   You tell me in your last letter (which gave me great
> pleasure) "I am a *baby*, learning to talk." Well, this last
> five or six weeks I am a baby too, for I live on nothing but
> *milk*, but I shall soon be taking my seat at the celestial
> banquet and quenching my thirst with the waters of eter-
> nal life! When you get this letter, without doubt I will
> have quit the earth...
>   *Au revoir*, my Brother, pray very much for your sister,
> *pray for our Mother*, whose sensitive and maternal heart
> has a hard time consenting to my departure. I count on
> you to console her.[47]

In her lasts words to Father Roulland Thérèse asks for prayers more insistently for the Prioress than for herself.

Thérèse never revealed her inner life to Adolphe Roulland. Nor did she permit herself to become attached to him.
At the start of their friendship Father Roulland gave her a
photograph of himself. Thérèse poured out her delight in a
letter as she used to pour out her delight to her father when
he brought treats to the Carmel.

[45]*Ibid.*, p. 984.
[46]DE, p. 162.
[47]Thérèse to P. Roulland, LT 254, July 14, 1897, CGII, pp. 1029, 30.

...it was with joy that our good Mother introduced *you* into the cloister. She allowed me to keep my brother's photograph, it is a *very special* privilege, a Carmelite does not have even the portraits of her nearest relations but Our Mother realized that yours, far from reminding me of the world and earthly affections, will raise my heart to regions far above...So, my Brother, while I shall cross the sea in your company you will stay close to me, well hidden in my poor cell...the picture you gave me lies always on my heart in the book of the Gospels, which never leaves me..."[48]

These warm words came from one who built her spiritual life on detachment; only because of this unbending and consistent habit could she write them. After she died, this note was found along with the photo:

"This photograph does not belong to me, our Mother told me to *keep it for her* in our writing-case, she will take it when she needs it."[49]

In a postscript to her long (1900 words) second letter to Father Roulland, Thérèse asked him to pray for "a young seminarian who wants to be a *missionary*; his vocation has been shaken by his year of military service."[50] This was Maurice Bellière, her first spiritual brother. In Thérèse's correspondence with Father Roulland she reassured him, took great interest in his life, and stilled his anxiety. In her correspondence with the Abbé Belière she clearly became his spiritual advisor. Maurice Bellière was wrestling with weakness and faults in himself, a struggle that Thérèse knew well: in her novices in Carmel, in Marie Guérin, in herself. After Maurice Bellière's initial contacts with the Carmel in the fall of 1895 came nine months of silence during which, he said later, he did some "extraordinarily foolish" things.[51] Ashamed

[48]Thérèse to P. Roulland, LT 193, July 30, 1896, CGII, pp. 875-6.
[49]Cl, p. 279, ft. 30.
[50]Thérèse to Père Roulland, Nov. 1, 1896, CLXXVIII, CL, p. 299.
[51]Piat, *Thérèse de Lisieux à la Découverte de la Voie D'Enfance,* p. 272.

of his behavior he still wanted to be a priest, but his confidence was shaken. Finally he wrote in the summer of 1896. Thérèse wrote him in October and again the day after Christmas in a rather stiff tone:

"I assure you, Monsieur l'Abbé, that I am doing all that lies in my power to obtain the graces you need; those graces will surely be granted, for Our Lord never asks us for sacrifices beyond our strength."[52]

Maurice Bellière wanted to be a missionary but recoiled from leaving his people.[53] In her next letter, remaining formal, Thérèse carefully reaches out to "Monsieur l'Abbé."

"I sense that our souls are made to understand each other. Your style, which you call 'coarse and unpolished,' reveals to me that Jesus has given your heart such aspirations as He gives only to souls called to the highest sanctity..."[54] He liked her poem *Vivre D'Amour;* she sent him others. And through a series of allusions she began to prepare this young seminarian for her death. "...if Jesus carries out my presentiments, I promise to remain your little sister up above..."[55] By the time she wrote her next letter all stiffness was gone: "My dear little Brother,

My pen, or rather my heart, refuses to go on calling you 'Monsieur l'Abbé' and our good Mother told me that in writing to you I could use the name I always use when I speak of you to Jesus..."[56] Now Thérèse writes to Maurice Bellière in her distinctive style—with warmth and the light touch of personal details, disguising as effectively as she did in her daily life in the Carmel the exhaustion caused by her coughing spells and fevers.

Her poetry opens discussion. The images of spear, helmet and armor in one of her poems amused him. "I smiled at the

---

[52]Thérèse to l'abbé Bellière, LT 213, Dec. 26, 1896, CGII, pp. 934-5.

[53]CL, p. 305, ft. 85.

[54]Thérèse to l'abbé Bellière, LT 220, Feb. 24, 1897, CGII, p. 951.

[55]*Ibid.,* p. 953.

[56]Thérèse to l'abbé Bellière, LT 224, April 25, 1897, CGII, p. 974.

thought of seeing you so armed..."[57] Thérèse replies:
"...as a child I dreamt of fighting on battlefields...Joan of Arc's exploits enchanted me;...it seemed to me that Our Lord destined me too for great things. I was not mistaken, but in place of voices from heaven inviting me to battle, I heard in the depths of my soul a voice sweeter, more powerful still...calling me to other exploits...in the solitude of Carmel I realized that my mission was not to get a mortal King crowned but to get the King of Heaven loved..."[58]

Thérèse detected in Maurice Bellière a common belief: the nuns in Carmel were all "great" souls; she lived in Carmel, therefore, in contrast to himself, she must be a great and perfect soul. She writes:

"My dear little Brother,

I must confess that in your letter there is one thing that pains me, it is that you do not know me as I am in reality...believe me, I beg you, the good God did not give you a *great* soul for your sister, but one that is *very small* and very imperfect."[59]

During May and June of that final year the treatment for Thérèse's illness involved cauterizations of her back with hot needles and blistering with hot plasters.[60] On Saturday, June 5th, Marie Guérin wrote home that they planned to take her picture because "by the end of the week her appearance would be so bad, it would be impossible to dream of doing this..."[61] The following Wednesday morning Thérèse received a long letter from Maurice Bellière containing a dramatic shift in mood. He began, "I have never chanted with more enthusiasm than yesterday the first stanza of the canticle of Love." He planned to leave the first of October for Algeria to train as a missionary. But the letter closed with the attitude Thérèse detected more and more—self-laceration.

[57]l'abbé Bellière to Thérèse, LC 177, April 17 or 18, 1897, CGII, p. 972.
[58]*Ibid.*, p. 976.
[59]*Ibid.*, p. 975.
[60]DE, pp. 32 and 148.
[61]Marie Guérin to Isidore Guérin, June 5, 1897, LA, p. 271.

"...How I must bore you, distract you...with all this verbiage in which it seems that I speak of myself to excess—pardon me—in truth, I assure you, I am a wretch..."[62] Exhausted, fighting sharp pains in her side, Thérèse wrote him a farewell letter that very day.[63] But as she felt better the next day she did not send it. On June 21 Thérèse wrote at length to calm the troubled young seminarian:

"O, my dear little Brother, please never think you 'bore me or distract me', by speaking much about yourself. Would it be possible for a sister not to take an interest *in all* that touches her brother?...Don't think you can frighten me with talk of 'your best years wasted.'" Dropping all the commonly used delicate phrases of her day, Thérèse bluntly warns him against spending his life punishing himself.

"I know there are saints who spent their lives in the practice of astonishing mortifications to expiate their sins, but what of it?—'In my Father's house there are many dwellings.' Jesus has told us so, which is why I follow the way He traces for me. I try to be occupied with myself in nothing..." Due to Magdalen's "loving audacity", Thérèse reminds him, Jesus' "...heart was disposed not only to pardon her but actually to lavish on her the favors of His divine intimacy and raise her to the highest summits of contemplation." She did not blame him for repenting of his sins and for wanting to expiate them. But she tried to prevent his brooding. "...you know, now that there are *two* of us the work will go faster and I, with *my way,* will get more done than you...so I hope that one day Jesus will set you on the same way as me."[64]

Maurice Bellière did not know about the unmailed letter of June 9 in which Thérèse, believing she was dying soon, wrote to say goodbye. Floundering as he was, her animated letters conveyed only strength. In a letter to the Prioress written two days before Thérèse was carried to the infirmary

[62]l'abbé Bellière to Thérèse, LC 186, June 7, 1897, CGII, pp. 1011 & 1013.

[63]CL, p. 343, ft. 83.

[64]Thérèse to l'abbé Bellière, LT 247, June 21, 1897, CGII, 1020-21.

(she was too weak to stand), Maurice Bellière asked that Thérèse write more frequently during his summer vacation, as her letters did so much for him.[65] A week later she wrote him:

"...the Spouse is at the door. It would take a miracle to keep me here in exile, and I do not think Jesus will work so pointless a miracle...You asked in your last letter to Our Mother that I write you often during vacation. If the Lord wills to prolong my pilgrimage by a few weeks more, I shall manage to scrawl more little notes like this, but most probably I shall be doing better than writing to my dear little Brother...I shall be *very near* him, I shall see all he needs, and I shall give the good God no rest till He has given me all I want!"[66]

Finally grasping that his cheerful correspondent is dying, Maurice Bellière is stunned by what he termed this "blow."[67] As sick as she was, Thérèse wrote him three more long letters. Even after her last letter to her sister Léonie,[68] to Father Roulland, and to the Aunt and Uncle who helped to raise her Thérèse continued to write to this struggling seminarian whom she never met. He pours out his anxiety and she writes back warmly, reassuringly, lovingly, never mentioning her own pain. With apparent ease Thérèse steps out of herself and into his point of view:

"O my little brother, how I would like to be able to pour into your heart the balm of consolation!...from your letter of the 14th my heart thrilled tenderly as I understood more than ever the degree to which your soul is sister to mine, since it is called to lift itself to God by the *elevator* of love and not to climb the rough staircase of fear..." He has difficulty with the practice of "familiarity" with Jesus. "...you cannot come to it in a day, but I am certain that I shall aid you better to walk that delightful way when I am

[65]CGII, p. 1028, ft. a, and LA, p. 79.

[66]Thérèse to l'abbé Bellière, LT 253, July 13, 1897, p. 1027.

[67]l'abbé Bellière to Thérèse, LC 189, July 17, 1897, CGII, p. 1037.

[68]With the exception of one brief thank you note written in August.

free of my mortal envelope. . ." She writes him a parable of two "mischievous and disobedient" sons awaiting punishment. While one stands "far off and trembling with terror, carrying in the depth of his heart the feeling that he deserves to be punished", the other casts himself into his father's arms saying that he loves him and will be good, and asks the father "to *punish* him with a *kiss*. . .(The father) does not ignore. . .that many a time his son will fall into the same faults, but he is ready to pardon him always, if always his son takes him by the heart."[69]

Too weak to control a pen, Thérèse wrote now in pencil.[70] The medical journal for July 26th notes that her hand trembled,[71] yet her long letter to Maurice Bellière that day glows with such warmth that one has difficulty imagining that the author was dying from tuberculosis:

"My dear little Brother,

What pleasure your letter gave me! If Jesus has heard your prayers and prolonged my exile. . . He has also granted mine, as you are resigned to lose 'my presence, my sensitive effect' as you call it. . . please, my brother, don't imitate the Hebrews who missed 'the onions of Egypt. . .'" Raw onions make you weep. ". . . Your soul is too great to be attached to any comfort here below."[72]

But Maurice Bellière was worried. Thérèse's confidence in him flows from ignorance—he has written her about his "faults" only vaguely, generally. He fears that if she knew all his misery it would chill her affection. "If you knew what a wretch I am!" He warns her against hearing the truth about him in heaven; she must close Jesus' mouth.[73] But to Thérèse one's faults were never abstract. They were always as particular as Magdalen's and never interfered with love, either hers or the Lord's.

[69]Thérèse to l'abbé Bellière, LT 258, July 18, 1897, CGII, pp. 1040 & 1041.

[70]DE, p. 159.

[71]DE, P. 165.

[72]Thérèse to l'abbé Bellière, LT 261, July 26, 1897, CGII, pp. 1051 & 1052.

[73]L'abbé Bellière to Thérèse, LC 191, July 21, 1897, CGII, p. 1044.

"You must know me very imperfectly," Thérèse wrote back, "to fear that a detailed account of your faults would diminish the tenderness that I have for your soul! O my brother, do you believe that I need to 'put my hand over Jesus' mouth.' He has long forgotten your infidelities...I beg you, never again *drag* yourself to His *feet*,' follow 'the first impulse which draws you into His arms': that is where you belong, and I see even more clearly than in your other letters, that you are *barred* from going to Heaven by any other way than your poor little sister's"[74]

Having opened his soul to a woman he has seen only in a photograph Maurice Bellière is curious. He doesn't even know her real name. He would like to know if it is Geneviève, but in his self-effacing way asks pardon for the "indiscretion" of asking a Carmelite to reveal something so personal.

"I find your question perfectly natural," Thérèse responded, and quite simply told him not only her name but details of her family and the story of her entering the Carmel. She wants him to be simple with God and with her, too. She was, she reminded him, his *sister*.[75]

The first week in August, 1897, Thérèse was tormented by vomiting blood, night sweats, nightmares and pain. After August 5th she again rallied. On August 7th Thérèse received a letter from Maurice Bellière. Still he is tortured by what he has done. When she is with God,

"...every stain must become an object of horror for you—That is why I am afraid..."[76] Still he is less conscious of her painful day to day existence than his own torment. Three days later Thérèse wrote Maurice Bellière for the last time. Avoiding any mention of her own pain, as always, she focuses fully on him.

"I believe that the Blessed have a great compassion for our wretchedness; they remember that when they were frail and

---

[74]Thérèse to l'abbé Bellière, July 26, 1897, CCXXXI, Cl, pp. 362-3.

[75]*Ibid.*, p. 1053.

[76]L'abbé Bellière to Thérèse, LC 193, Aug. 5, 1897, CGII, p. 1059.

mortal like us they committed the same faults, endured the same struggles. . ."[77] He wants Thérèse's crucifix to remind him of her when she is gone. In her final letter we see Thérèse's understanding of this natural desire and how gently she suggests the ideal of detachment.

"Now, my little brother, I must tell you of the *inheritance* you will receive after my death. Here is part of what our Mother will give you: first, the reliquary that I received the day of my taking of the habit and which has never left me—secondly, a small Crucifix which is incomparably dearer to me than the large one for the one I have now is not the first one given to me. At the Carmel, we sometimes exchange objects of piety as a good means of preventing growing attached to them." He would also receive the last picture she painted. He had asked if she became his sister "by choice or by chance." In the margin of her last letter she wrote:

"It was by choice that I became your sister."[78] A final act of kindness, for it was not her own choice, but Pauline's.

There is a postscript to the story of Thérèse's relationship with priests. Father Pichon, whom she asked to be her spiritual advisor before entering the Carmel and who was now in Canada, did not write to her during the final months of her ordeal, though she wrote him a long letter during the last summer. Finally he wrote a letter, buoyant, but brief and impersonal. ". . . The day you leave for heaven (for I suspect you very strongly of wanting to leave us) stretch your hands toward Canada to take all my messages. . ." The letter was dated October 4th, the day she was buried.[79]

Maurice Bellière harnessed his self doubt and left for Algeria to join the seminary the day before she died. Three days later he, too, wrote a letter not knowing Thérèse was

[77]Thérèse to l'abbé Bellière, Aug. 10, 1897, CGII, p. 1061.

[78]Thérèse to l'abbé Bellière, Aug. 10, 1897, CCXXV, CL, p. 368. See ft. 139.

[79]P. Pichon to Thérèse, LC, 202, October 4, 1897, CGII, p. 1084.

dead. Maurice Bellière's was a rambling, personal and jubilant letter. "My dear and very dear little Sister, be happy; the soul which you love so much and for which you have dispensed prayers and good works has realized finally—or at any rate nearly entirely—your most precious desires. Your brother, little sister, is a missionary since yesterday...."[80]

[80]l'abbé Bellière to Thérèse, LC, 201, October 2, 1897, CG II, p. 1082.

VIII

Darkness and Trust

"...my way is all of trust and love, I don't understand souls who fear so tender a Friend..."[1]
Thérèse to Père Roulland, May, 1897.

"During those very joyful days of the Easter season... He permitted my soul to be invaded by the thickest darkness...the thought of heaven, up until then so sweet to me,...(was) no longer anything but the cause of struggle and torment."[2]
Thérèse, June, 1897

A few weeks after she wrote to Père Roulland that her "way is all of trust and love" Thérèse took up again her copybook of memories, this time to provide Mother Marie de Gonzague with material for her obituary letter to the other Carmels. Writing under obedience to her Prioress within four months of her death, Thérèse now described what no one, not even Pauline, had guessed: her cheerfulness

[1]Thérèse to P. Roulland, LT 226, May 9, 1897, GC II, 984.
[2]C, p. 211.

masked a virtually constant inner struggle against the "thickest darkness."

The darkness had descended quite abruptly 14 months earlier at Easter time, just a few days after the first vomiting of blood convinced her that she would very likely die young. It is risky to assume an understanding of just what she experienced, for when Thérèse tried to explain it on paper she found it "impossible."

"One would have to travel through this dark tunnel to understand its darkness."[3] She tried a comparison. Since Thérèse herself shunned the reduction of experience to commonly used expressions, the story she chose to cast indirect light on her conflict merits being quoted at length:

> I imagine I was born in a country which is covered in thick fog. I never had the experience of contemplating the joyful appearance of nature flooded and transformed by the brilliance of the sun. It is true that from childhood I have heard people speak of these marvels, and I know the country in which I am living is not really my true fatherland, and there is another I must long for without ceasing. This is not simply a story invented by someone living in the sad country where I am, but it is a reality, for the King of the Fatherland of the bright sun actually came and lived for thirty-three years in the land of darkness...
>
> ...the certainty of going away one day far from the sad and dark country had been given me from the day of my childhood... I felt that another land would one day serve me as a permanent dwelling place. Then suddenly the fog which surrounds me becomes more dense; it penetrates my soul and envelops it in such a way that it is impossible to discover within it the sweet image of my Fatherland; everything has disappeared! When I want to rest my heart fatigued by the darkness which surrounds it by the memory of the luminous country after which I aspire, my torment redoubles; it seems to me that the darkness, bor-

[3]C, p. 212.

rowing the voice of sinners, says mockingly to me: "You are dreaming about the light, about a fatherland embalmed in the sweetest perfumes; you are dreaming about the *eternal* possession of the Creator of all these marvels; you believe that one day you will walk out of this fog which surrounds you! Advance, advance; rejoice in death which will give you not what you hope for but a night still more profound, the night of nothingness." Dear Mother, the image I wanted to give you for the darkness that obscures my soul is as imperfect as a sketch is to the model; however I don't want to write any longer about it; I fear I might blaspheme; I fear even that I have already said too much.[4]

As she wrote these lines Thérèse knew well that they would baffle Mother Marie de Gonzague. Thérèse *appeared* so happy. Her poetry, read often at Carmel celebrations, resonated with a sweet and intimate faith. In December 1896, she composed this poem:

Divine Savior, at the close of my life
Come search for me without a shadow of delay
Ah! show me your endless tenderness
And the sweetness of your divine glance.
With love, oh! how your voice calls to me
Saying to me: Come, all is pardoned
Rest yourself, my faithful spouse
Come to my heart, much have you loved me.[5]

[4]C, pp. 212-13.
[5]"Comment je veux aimer," *Poésies,* p. 194.
This is the third and last stanza of the poem:
Divin Sauveur, à la fin de ma vie
Viens me chercher, sans l'ombre d'un retard
Ah! montre-moi ta tendresse infinie
Et la douceur de ton divin regard
Avec amour, oh! que ta voix m'appelle
En me disant; Viens, tout est pardonné
Repose-toi, mon épouse fidèle
Viens sur mon coeur, tu ma'as beaucoup aimé.

The darkness had invaded Thérèse nearly nine months before she wrote this poem.

"My dear Mother," she addressed the Prioress the following June, "I may perhaps appear to you to be exaggerating my trial. In fact, if you are judging according to the sentiments I express in my little poems composed this year, I must appear to you as a soul filled with consolations and one for whom the veil of faith is almost torn aside; and yet it is no longer a veil for me, it is a wall...When I sing of the happiness of heaven and of the eternal possession of God, I feel no joy in this, for I sing simply what *I WANT TO BELIEVE*..."⁶ Whatever the Prioress's reaction might be, Thérèse made no effort either to rationalize the apparent contradiction or to soften the truth. Never did she trim life as she experienced it to fit an ideal. The final summer she told Pauline,

"We should never make any false currency in order to redeem souls."⁷ And so while her sisters spoke around her bed of visions and ecstasies accompanying her death Thérèse herself felt nothing, imagined nothing.

* * * * *

To understand how Thérèse could write such buoyant poetry and support Maurice Bellière with such strength while she herself battled inner darkness in the face of death, we must examine more precisely the words she used. Thérèse's style is simple and fresh; while she drew on the vocabulary of her tradition, she did not restrict herself to words and phrases which all around her assumed they understood in the same way. For example, her letters of the last seven years of her life as a contemplative nun yield only one use of the word "contemplation" and nineteen of the verb "to contemplate," yet the verb "to hide" appears approximately 55 times. She liked to write of action: while the noun "hope" appears only 12 times the verb "to hope" appears nearly one

⁶C, p. 214.
⁷LA, p. 82.

hundred times. We see the verbs "to believe," "to desire," "to understand," "to remain," "to console," all appearing frequently in her letters. The rather vague adjective "heroic" which figured so significantly in the questions asked during the Process investigating her sanctity, appears only 3 times, and faith *(foi)*, only 7 times.[8] Turning back to Thérèse's description of what happened when that wall of darkness descended we find her alluding to "faith", the standard word appearing often in the liturgy, readings and sermons of her day:

"...at this time I was enjoying such a living faith, such a clear *faith,* that the thought of heaven made up all my happiness, and I was unable to believe there were really impious people who had no faith."[9]

But another word appears regularly in her copybook of memories, a word far less familiar to the ear of the Catholic of her day than either faith or hope: *confiance,* translated confidence or trust. The use of *confiance* is a significant example of Thérèse's departing from received language to choose a word less traditional but more precise to describe her experience. In her writing during the last two years of her life appear four striking occurrences of *confiance.*

The first time Thérèse is describing the event now familiar to us which occurred after three and one half years in the Carmel. Agonizing over her "faults," worried that she was continuously offending God, doubting the existence of heaven, Thérèse poured out her grief during the retreat of 1891 to Father Alexis Prou:

"After speaking only a few words, I *was understood* in a marvelous way and my soul was like a book in which this priest read better than I did myself. He launched me full sail upon the waves of *confidence and love* which so strongly attracted me, but upon which I dared not advance.. My

[8]For this count I rely on the "Index des Mots Principaux des Lettres de Thérèse", CG II, pp. 1351-1390. The word "hope" encompasses both *espoir* and *espérance.*
[9]C, p. 211.

nature was such that fear made me recoil..."[10]

The word *confiance* also appears in her Act of Oblation to Merciful Love, written in June of 1895, in which Thérèse offered herself as Victim to God's Love:

"...I am certain, then, that you will grant my desires; I know, O my God! that *the more You want to give, the more You make us desire*. I feel in my heart immense desires and it is with confidence I ask You to come and take possession of my soul..."[11]

A third significant occurrence is in her impassioned letter to her sister Marie in 1896 in which Thérèse recounts her moment of discovery: "MY VOCATION IS LOVE." As her feelings for Jesus rush from her, Thérèse writes:

"O, Jesus, allow me in my boundless gratitude to say to You that Your *love reaches unto folly*. In the presence of this folly, how can You not desire that my heart leap towards You? How can my confidence, then, have any limits?..."[12]

Finally, her last copybook, the one addressed to Mother Marie de Gonzague in June, 1897 in which she described her inner darkness, ends abruptly with this broken thought:

> Most of all I imitate the conduct of Magdalene; her astonishing or rather her loving audacity which charms the Heart of Jesus also attracts my own. Yes, I feel it; even though I had on my conscience all the sins that can be committed, I would go, my heart broken with sorrow, and throw myself into Jesus' arms, for I know how much He loves the prodigal child who returns to Him. It is not because God, in His anticipating Mercy, has preserved my soul from mortal sin that I go to Him with confidence and love...[13]

[10]A, pp. 173-4.

[11]SS, p. 276.

[12]B, p. 200.

[13]C, p. 259.

A few weeks before Thérèse died, Pauline was sitting by her bed during the noon silence. Thérèse pointed outside at a row of chestnut trees.

"Look! Do you see the black hole...where we can see nothing; it's in a similar hole that I am as far as body and soul are concerned...what darkness! But I am in peace."[14] To grasp how Thérèse faced death in peace despite the dark hole, we must examine the sense in which "faith" was commonly understood.

*   *   *   *   *

In her copybook of memories Thérèse jotted down her thoughts as they came to her, without headings. After Thérèse died, to make her copybook more readable when it was published Pauline divided it into sections. To the one in which Thérèse wrote of her "inner darkness" Pauline assigned the title "The Trial of Faith."[15] In her groping to explain her inner darkness to Mother Marie de Gonzague Thérèse had termed it simply a "trial," avoiding, as usual, any expression so common it bordered on cliché:
"I would like to be able to express what I feel, but...I believe this is impossible. One would have to travel through this dark tunnel to understand its darkness..."
The words "Trial of Faith" in bold print at the start of this section stamped Thérèse's "inner darkness" with the popular notion of what a "trial of faith" meant. Faith was understood primarily as unquestioned belief, frequently unquestioned belief in God. In Thérèse's milieu it was also synonymous with belief in Catholicism, the Catholic *Faith*. One suffering a "trial of Faith" might be doubting God, the

---

[14]LA, p. 173.
[15]C, p. 212.
The phrase appears in Thérèse's poem "Mon Ciel a Moi!"
"...Mon Jesus me sourit quand vers Lui je soupire,
Alors je ne sens plus l'épreuve de la foi...
Thérèse does not particularly call attention to this phrase and she does not capitalize it.
Poésies: un Cantigue d'amour. p. 170.

Church, or specific doctrinal truths that were to be accepted without necessarily being understood. In this last, restricted sense, though Pauline's phrase drastically oversimplified Thérèse's inner state, it was accurate. Thérèse doubted; specifically, she doubted heaven.

But the primary meaning of the Latin root word *fides* was not belief but trust: "The condition of having trust placed in one, trust, tutelage," according to the modern Oxford Latin dictionary. "Belief, conviction" is listed as the twelfth definition. The verb is *fidere,* and *confidere* meant "to put one's trust in, have confidence in." [16] In French *confiance* expresses confidence *(confidentia)* or personal trust. *Confiance* is the word that appears so significantly in Thérèse's writing during the last two years of her life.

In his *Two Types of Faith* Martin Buber explains that the distinctive faith of the people of Israel was not the acknowledging of something as true but a relationship of trust in a person. This type of faith "arises from the fact that I trust someone, without being able to offer sufficient reasons for my trust in him. . ." [17] According to the *New Catholic Encyclopedia* the most common Hebrew root employed to express Israel's attitude to God is *'mn* of which the basic meaning is "firmness, certainty, reliability, trustworthiness.." ". . . Israel's faith was closely connected with the idea of trust in Yahweh. . ." [18]

Thérèse was exposed to Biblical passages in Latin, in French translation filtered through both Latin *and* Greek, and to the psalms translated directly from the original Hebrew. The differences disturbed her, according to Cèline. Without knowing the ancient languages she could not

[16] *Oxford Latin Dictionary.* (Oxford: Clarendon Press, 1968), pp. 697, 698, 400. *Confiance* derives from the Latin, *confidentia;* in Old French *fiance* meant "faith". Paul Robert, *Le Petit Robert, Dictionnaire Alphabetique et analogique de la langue* française. (Paris: Sociéte du Nouveau Littré, 1969).

[17] Martin Buber, *Two Types of Faith,* (N.Y.: Harper & Row, 1951), p. 7. See also Norman Lamm, "Faith and Doubt," in *Faith and Doubt: Studies in Traditional Jewish Thought,* (NY: KTAV Publishing House Inc., 1971), pp. 1-34;

[18] *New Catholic Encyclopedia,* vol. 3, (NY: McGraw-Hill, 1967), p. 793.

determine which translation rendered precisely the original text.[19] In Sacy's French translation the word *espérance* permeates the psalms. *Espérance* is based on the Latin root word *spes* ("a feeling or state of hope, expectation of something desired").

A sharp distinction exists between the Hebrew denoting "hope" (which also translates "wait for" and does not appear very often), and the characters used to convey the notion of *trust* appearing so regularly in the psalms. But the Latin Vulgate generally employs *Spero* (I hope) for the Hebrew "I trust", and *Exspecto* for "I hope." In French this becomes *J'espere* and *J'attend* (I hope, I wait). The meaning of *trust*, so vital to the Hebrews, is lost.

Comparing passages of psalms translated directly from the Hebrew texts with the Latin Vulgate and the French 19th century Sacy translation reveals the difference this translation makes. (The Hebrew numbering is one ahead of the Latin and French, and there is some variation, too, in the numbering of passages.) A nearly literal translation from the Hebrew of Psalm 56:3, 4 reads:

> Raise me up when I am most afraid,
> I put my trust in you;
> . . .
> In God I put my trust, fearing nothing;
> what can men do to me?[20]

In the same passage in the Latin Vulgate trust is translated *sperabo* the first time, *speravi* the second. The Sacy French translation, based on the Latin, reads:

---

[19]The Carmel had a copy of the Sacy translation which contained the Psalms but omitted several other books of the Old Testament. *(La Bible avec Thérèse de Lisieux,* p. 309.) Though not all the nuns had free access to it, French translations of passages chanted in choir were read aloud. Céline's hand-copied Bible which she gave to Thérèse in 1894 was translated by Glaire. Thérèse's *Manuel du Chiétian* contained the psalms translated from the original Hebrew. Gaucher, *La Bible avec Thérèse de Lisieux*, p. 310.

[20]*The Jerusalem Bible,* (Garden City, N.J., 1968), p. 724.

> I will hope in you (J'espérerai),
> ...I have put my hope in God. (55:3, 4)[21]

Similarly, Psalm 36:3 reads in the 19th century French translation:

> Put your hope in the Lord, and do good;
> And then you will inhabit the land, and be nourished with its riches.[22]

The message of the original Hebrew text:

> Trust in Yahweh and do what is good,
> make your home in the land and live in peace. (37:3)[23]

Though the meaning of Hebrew and French words can vary according to context, the Latin word *spes* clearly has the connotation of expectation, of hope in the future. It is distinct from the stress on the present conveyed by *confidere*, to trust. Thérèse's own *confiance* expressed most precisely the original Hebrew meaning. She lived in the continuing personal trust expressed over and over again by these ancient poets. When she doubted a belief she had been taught, when the dark night descended, like the psalmist she still "trusted in him."

When Thérèse wrote of inner darkness obscuring the Fatherland and voices mocking her desire for "*eternal* possession of the Creator," she described doubting a particular belief: eternal life. Another source on Thérèse's doubts suggests a problem equally common to the modern mind. Pauline describes Thérèse at the close of her life as tempted by "the reasoning of the worst materialists...(that in time) science will explain everything naturally; we shall have the absolute reason for everything that exists..." In her intellectual doubts, in her concern that science might eventually

[21]Le Maistre de Sacy, Translator, *La Sainte Bible,* (Paris: Garnier Freres, 1875), p. 657. The Glaire translation also employs *jèspérerai,* I shall hope. In the *Manuel du Chrétien* (1864) both *jèspére* and *confiance* appear in the passage.

[22]Le Maistre de Sacy, p. 646. The Glaire translation: "Espère dans le Seigneur..." The Manuel du Chrétien: Espérez dans le Seigneur...".

[23]*The Jerusalem Bible,* (Garden City, N.J. 1968) p. 706.

explain away everything, Thérèse was very much a child of her times. In the 1890's, prior to pollution and the Bomb, unbounded faith in science was common. Thérèse also was concerned that after her death nothing would happen; she would never do the good she wished to do. "It will be as it was for Mother Geneviève: we expected to see her work miracles, and complete silence fell over her tomb..."[24] Pauline may have found Thérèse's doubts unsettling; she did not include this report in her initial publication of Thérèse's last conversations. She learned of these specific difficulties only a month before Thérèse died. "Up until then," Pauline said, "I had known of her trial of faith only vaguely."[25] With her usual self-discipline Thérèse had kept her inner struggle to herself. "She spoke to nobody about it," Céline explained, "for fear she would pass her own...torment on to them..."[26] How is one to make sense, then, of the behavior that astonished all who watched her die so slowly and painfully during her final four months? She appeared always calm, never as one battling within herself.

"Thérèse has spent a very bad night," her aunt wrote to her cousin five days before Thérèse died. "This morning, she's as usual...Dr. De Cornière was admiring his patient's gentleness and patience. It seems she's suffering atrociously. He can't understand how she continues to live..."[27] Thérèse embodied a critical distinction: while unable to believe without question *that* she would soon live with her Spouse forever, she continued to have confidence *in* God. [28]

Without realizing it, Thérèse linked ancient and modern insights. Because her approach to God is not static but a continuous encounter Thérèse has been compared with Martin Buber who addressed God as I/Thou. To Henri Bergeson she represented the spiritual *elan* at the heart of his

[24]LA, p. 258.

[25]LA, p. 257.

[26]TE, p. 123.

[27]Madame Guérin to Madame La Neele, September 25, 1897, in LA, p. 291.

[28]See Lamm, pp. 1-34.

philosophy. Thérèse's habit of living "from instant to instant" suggests the modern existentialist viewpoint; many consider doubt basic to the existentialist experience. But her doubt remained confined to specific beliefs, and in her powerful trust *despite* the doubts, despite the darkness, Thérèse never succumbed to the "dread" described by Kierkegaard. As she shunned the religion of fear and the perfectionism and static phrases she inherited from the past, she shunned too, the deep *malaise* of the modern era. Her counterpoint to the poison of anxiety was not a faith centered merely on intellectual assent but a relationship with God based on personal trust. *Trust* formed the basis of her message to Pauline ever anxious at her bedside, *trust* formed the basis of her message to Father Roulland fearing Purgatory, and *trust* formed the basis of her message to the abbé Bellière wrestling with his shame.

In her May, 1897 letter to Father Roulland, Thérèse berates him a bit for doubting his "immediate entry into heaven" if he were murdered.

"...the Lord is infinitely just and it is this justice which terrifies so many souls that is the basis of my joy and trust...my way is all of trust and love, I don't understand those souls who fear so tender a Friend."[29]

Thérèse's words echo the ancient refrain of the Israelites as well as Christians: trust in him. She was not original; she saw what had been there from ancient times. But the purity of this strain of tradition was clouded in her day by the habit of assumed understanding of faith as repeated over centuries: belief or intellectual assent. It would be a distortion to suggest that Thérèse rejected the importance of belief. She developed no such theological position and her doubts troubled her deeply. Clearly Thérèse desired the complete and unquestioned belief that eluded her toward the end of her life. She discussed her doubts with Father Youf, the chaplain, who warned her not to dwell on them as they were

---

[29]Thérèse to P. Roulland, LT 226, May 9, 1897, GC II, pp. 983 and 984.

"dangerous."[30] Céline has testified that Thérèse followed the advice of another priest:

"...she copied the Creed, and carried it around with her; she was prepared to write it with her blood."[31] While Thérèse did not take her doubts lightly, she refused to let anxiety engulf her, torment her, banish her trust in the God she was dying for, even during the hemorrhages and suffocation and fevers of her last monotonous summer when God was silent.

* * * * *

Judging from her buoyant letters to Maurice Bellière it would seem that this trust never deserted Thérèse. But she wrote those letters on her good days, and the letters stopped altogether on August 10th, seven weeks before she finally died. How did her trust hold up on the bad days?

"Oh, what a feeling I have that you're going to suffer!" Pauline said on July 4th.

"What does it matter!" said Thérèse. "...I'm sure God will never abandon me."[32]

Three and a half weeks later began a period of 8 days of intense fever and vomiting of blood.[33] The right lung was now "totally lost, filled with tubercles in the process of softening," according to a medical report, and the left lung was also affected.[34] Thérèse labored to breathe, a sight painful for Pauline to watch. Once again Pauline could not contain her own "sorrow."

"Don't be disturbed;" Thérèse told her. "if I can't breathe, God will give me the strength to bear it. I love him! He'll never abandon me."[35] Three days later Thérèse received the last rites of the Church. The next day doctor predicted that she would live another month or more.

[30]TE, p. 123.
[31]*Ibid.*
[32]LA, p. 73.
[33]DE, pp. 166-7.
[34]Dr. Francis La Néele to M. Guérin, August 26, 1897, LA, p. 290.
[35]LA, p. 115.

"What does it matter?" she said...God will give me strength; He'll never abandon me."[36] Three weeks later "she was seized with terrible intestinal pains and her stomach was as hard as a rock...she said the pain was enough to make her lose her reason."[37] Thérèse asked Pauline not to leave any poisonous medications around her.[38]

That night was the worst she had yet spent.[39] The next day Thérèse said,

"Never would I believe I could suffer so much. And yet I believe I'm not at the end of my pains; but he will not abandon me."[40] Five weeks later, still alive, Thérèse told Sister Marie of the Trinity in a voice sounding "strangled," that she was surprised there were not more suicides among atheists. Sister Marie said Thérèse tried to smile at her, and appeared "calm."[41]

She died at 7:20 on Thursday evening, the 30th of September. By all accounts her final day was appalling unrelieved pain.[42] During that last day Thérèse cried out to God,

"...have pity on Your poor little child! Have pity on her!"[43] She was, we must remember, only 24. She turned to the Prioress, Mother Marie de Gonzague who had replaced Pauline at her bedside:

"O Mother, I assure you, the chalice is filled to the brim!..."

"But God is not going to abandon me, I'm sure..."

"He has never abandoned me."[44]

With hindsight we know that within hours her torture

[36]LA, pp. 123-4.
[37]LA, ft. pp. 162-3.
[38]LA, p. 163.
[39]LA, p. 164.
[40]*Ibid.*
[41]TE, p. 254.
[42]DE, p. 555.
[43]LA, p. 205.
[44]*Ibid.*

ended. But Thérèse herself had no such certainty. Earlier in the day, according to Pauline,

"She appeared to be at the end of her strength and never-theless, to our great surprise, she was able to move, to sit up in her bed.

"You see the strength that I have today! No, I'm not going to die! I still have strength for months, perhaps years. . ."[45] Right up to the point of her death Thérèse had no certainty that her suffering would end quickly or earn her any reward. She faced the darkness with only the trust of Job.

[45]LA, p. 204.

IX

Love

"...He has no need of our works but only of our love..."[1]
Thérèse, 1897

"Ah! Lord, I know you don't command the impossible... You know very well that never would I be able to love my Sisters as You love them, unless *You*, O my Jesus, *loved them in me.*"[2]
Thérèse, 1897

In June, 1895, Thérèse took her sister Céline to a little room adjoining her cell, knelt and read the formal statement of about 600 words in which she offered herself as a Holocaust to God's Love.

"...I desire," it began, "to *Love* You and make You *Loved*...

> I know, O my God! that *the more You want to give, the more You make us desire*. I feel in my heart immense desires and it is with confidence I ask You to come and

[1] B, p. 189.
[2] C, p. 221.

take possession of my soul...Remain in me as in a tabernacle...

I want to console You for the ingratitude of the wicked ...If through weakness I sometimes fall, may Your *Divine Glance* cleanse my soul immediately, consuming all my imperfections like the fire that transforms everything into itself...In order to live in one single act of perfect Love, I OFFER MYSELF AS A VICTIM OF HOLOCAUST TO YOUR MERCIFUL LOVE, asking You to consume me incessantly, allowing the waves of *infinite tenderness* shut up within You to overflow into my soul, and that thus I may become a *martyr* of Your Love,...[3]

Thérèse's prayer seems steeped in a different age. In the same year that Céline Martin introduced photography to the cloister, Thérèse presented herself as a holocaust, a burnt offering to God. In fact this act is the peak of Thérèse's insight; it sets her apart from believers shackled to an Old Law view of appeasing a just God and aligns her firmly with the New Law. Not only does she shed the archaic remnants very much alive in her companions in the monastery, but by this act even more than she understood herself as she knelt in the small room, she resolved the central conflict in her life and the conflict of many modern people drawn to God.

In Thérèse's time the idea of appeasement held many Catholics in its grip: we are guilty and should fear God's just retribution. In this view Christ's crucifixion was initially an act of appeasement to God's Justice: the Lamb took upon himself the punishment for sinners. Indeed, the stark Carmelite life of prayer and penance lived to the letter by so many of her sisters within the Lisieux community was understood to deflect God's anger and punishment from sinners.[4] Even Mother Geneviève, the Foundress, whose

---

[3]SS, pp. 276-7.

[4]Piat, *St. Thérèse de Lisieux à la Découverte de la Voie d'Enfance*, p. 79. The tone of appeasement is clear from some of the entries quoted by Piat from the *Treasure of the Carmel*.

simplicity Thérèse loved, offered herself to God's Justice.[5]

But this idea, the one still more dramatic sacrifice open to her from the tradition of the order, other than being a missionary, held no appeal for Thérèse.

"I was thinking about the souls who offer themselves as victims of God's Justice in order to turn away the punishments reserved to sinners," she wrote early in 1896, "drawing them upon themselves. This offering seemed great and very generous to me, but I was far from feeling attracted to it."[6] In offering herself to God Thérèse integrates her own distinctive path with the core of the tradition as she had come to understand it. "...the road that leads to this Divine Furnace...is the *surrender* of the little child who sleeps without fear in its Father's arms."[7] God does not seek vengeance; He is her Father. For her part, the self that she had begun to purge of all its whims, customs, tastes and dreams would be transformed not by achieving perfection through her own efforts, however extreme, but by the fire of God's love. She writes in her letter of September 1896 to Marie:

> I am only a child, powerless and weak, and yet it is my weakness that gives me the boldness of offering myself as *VICTIM of Your Love, O Jesus!* In times past, victims, pure and spotless, were the only ones accepted by the Strong and Powerful God. To satisfy Divine *Justice*, perfect victims were necessary, but the *law of Love* has succeeded to the law of fear, and *Love* has chosen me as a holocaust, me, a weak and imperfect creature. Is not this choice worthy of Love? Yes, in order that Love be fully satisfied, it is necessary that It lower Itself, and that It lower Itself to nothingness and transform this nothingness into *fire*...[8]

[5]Gaucher, *Histoire D'Une Vie*, p. 157.

[6]A, p. 180.

[7]B, p. 188.

[8]B, p. 195.

It is revealing to compare passages of this formal offering in 1895 to the letter she carried on her profession day five years earlier. The profession letter of September 8, 1890 contains the seeds of the distinctive path to God that Thérèse would develop over the next five years:

> Jesus, I ask You for nothing but peace, and also love, infinite love without any limits other than yourself; love which is no longer I but you, my Jesus... Let nobody be occupied with me, let me be... forgotten like Your little grain of sand...[9]

But at the age of 17 the ideals of perfection and martyrdom retained their hold on Thérèse:

> ... Take me before I can commit the slightest voluntary fault... Give me martyrdom of heart or of body, or rather give me both.[10]

The martyrdom she sought at age 22 was distinct from what she imagined at age 17. As we have seen in Chapter IV, the dramatic act of publicly dying for God no longer occupied the central place. In 1895 she prayed, "May this martyrdom, after having prepared me to appear before you, finally cause me to die..."[11] This was not a request to be burned at the stake: Thérèse was living the offering of herself daily as she was being purged by an interior "consuming fire."

The tone of the offering of herself to God's Love is far more confident than that of the letter written for her profession five years earlier:

> "I desire... to be a saint, but I feel my helplessness and I beg You, O my God! to be Yourself my *Sanctity*!... In the evening of this life, I shall appear before You with empty hands, for I do not ask You, Lord, to count my works. All our justice is stained in Your eyes. I wish, then

[9]SS, p. 275.
[10]*Ibid.*
[11]SS, p. 277.

to be clothed in Your own *Justice* and to receive from Your *Love* the eternal possession of *Yourself*. . ." [12]

By 1895 Thérèse was no longer tortured by her own continuous failure. She was sure of herself. The following May she wrote this familiar passage to Father Roulland:

". . .this justice which terrifies so many souls. . .is the basis of my joy and trust. . ." [13]

* * * * *

As Thérèse's letters and written memories disclose, she delineated her own personality and insights from those of the women with whom she lived, ordinary women, not quite the great and perfect souls Maurice Bellière imagined within those walls. Thérèse revered Mother Geneviève, the Foundress; but the Carmel also contained some difficult personalities, such as Sister Teresa of Saint Augustine, 39 years old in 1895, who Thérèse found "displeasing. . .in everything, in her ways, her words, her character, everything seems *very disagreeable* to me"; [14] and 44 year old Sister Aimée of Jesus, a foe of the Martin clan, who desired a community of seamstresses and nurses rather than painters and poets. Sister Aimée testified at the Process: "I was one of the instruments God made use of to sanctify. . .(Thérèse). The charitable way she bore with my defects brought her to an outstanding degree of holiness. . ." [15]

By the time she wrote the offering Thérèse was directing the novices, [16] each of whom had some problem that required patient attention. There was 21 year old Sister Marie of the Trinity, 13th of a family of 19, who cried easily, craved

---

[12]SS, pp. 276, 277.

[13]Thérèse to Pére Roulland, LT 226, May 9, 1897, CG II, p. 983.

[14]C, p. 222.

[15]TE, p. 279.

[16]Pauline appointed her to assist Mother Marie de Gonzague who held the title of Novice Mistress. Thérèse actually performed the duties of the office without the title. See TE, p. 31.

attention, and had left the Paris Carmel[17]; 24 year old Marie Guérin, Thérèse's cousin, who had suffered from scruples; 26 year old Mary Magdalen of the Blessed Sacrament, emotionally scarred from her childhood when she was sent out to work in a home at a very young age and was assaulted. She was "sombre, withdrawn and sullen to the point that they questioned whether to send her away;"[18] 30 year old Sister Martha of Jesus who spent her childhood in orphanages, and though a professed nun, remained by request with Thérèse in the Novitiate.[19] And, of course, Céline, whose "intense drive" to perfection Thérèse worked to temper. Each of these women lived the same disciplined life; there could be no doubt of the sincere dedication of each to the Carmelite ideal. Yet they could be cold, carping, self-justifying, critical.

"Look at the walk of her!" one of the Sisters said of Thérèse one day, loud enough to be overheard. "She's not in any hurry. When is she going to start working? She's good for nothing."[20] Devoted to their Saviour, their treatment of each other at times showed little trace of his strongest message. While each of these women performed her duties with vigor, some were frozen into neurotic personalities, while in others devotion to certain ideals and patterns of the religious life had displaced the core. Thérèse recognized the rigid clinging to external patterns as an obstacle to finding the deepest truth of the tradition.

In her letter of September, 1896 to Marie (in the form of addressing Jesus) Thérèse explained her final leap to a fully integrated vision. To live the core of Christ's message she must strip herself of any leftover dreams of dramatic "vocations." Leading up to this moment of insight, she described her "desires and longings" even there in the Carmel where she had made the great sacrifice of her life. "To be Your

[17]DE, pp. 861-2 and TE, p. 241.

[18]Piat, *St. Thérèse de Lisieux à la Découverte de la Voie d'Enfance*, p. 171.

[19]TE, p. 216.

[20]TE, p. 264.

Spouse, to be a *Carmelite,* and by my union with You to be *Mother* of souls, should not this suffice me? And yet it is not so."[21] In the absence of satisfaction, she had dreamed of other identities, other more dramatic ideals:
"...I feel within me other *vocations.* I feel the *vocation* of the WARRIOR, THE PRIEST, THE APOSTLE, THE DOCTOR, THE MARTYR..."[22] The heroic impulse to live life totally for God remained strong. But now Thérèse pieced together the interior need of the discontented souls about her with the necessity that she shed the idea of vocation as defined and confined within these fixed categories. The solution to what was missing in her role as "spouse, Carmelite, Mother" was not to reach beyond it to yet another fixed vocation, yet another map to guide her toward yet another ideal. What was missing in the core of her life at the Carmel could *also* be missing in the life of the priest and the life of the martyr. Without that element the most technically perfect person was incomplete, the most dramatic sacrifice was empty. Now turning from every particular ideal, be it Carmelite, Priest, Apostle or Martyr, Thérèse chose to "be" love, right where she was, there in the little Carmel among the hurt and rigid people so much in need of the core of Jesus' message.

> ...the Apostle explains how all *the most PERFECT gifts* are nothing without *LOVE.* That *Charity is the EXCELLENT WAY* that leads most surely to God.
> I finally had rest...
> *I understood it was Love alone* that made the Church's members act, that if *Love* ever became extinct, apostles would not preach the Gospel and martyrs would not shed their blood. I understood that LOVE COMPRISED ALL VOCATIONS, THAT LOVE WAS EVERYTHING, THAT IT EMBRACED ALL TIMES AND PLACES...IN A WORD, THAT IT WAS ETERNAL!
> Then, in the excess of my delirious joy, I cried out: O

---

[21]B, p. 192.
[22]*Ibid.*

Jesus, my Love...My *vocation,* at last I have found it...MY VOCATION IS LOVE!
...in the heart of the Church, my Mother, I shall be *Love.* Thus I shall be everything...[23]

*   *   *   *   *

Having arrived at the heart of Thérèse's vision we stand in danger of missing it. Her extravagant use of a word grown faded and vague from overuse in our day is an obstacle nearly as great as the haloed pictures. To overanalyze Thérèse's many uses of the word love would trivialize the mystery; but Thérèse herself consistently refused to retreat into mystery when something could be understood.

As happens with frequently quoted words, by Thérèse's time "charity" had taken on a static meaning. Regardless of the root meaning of the word, "charitable" acts were defined in external ways; "charity" often meant the giving of alms. It was possible, in the quantitative method that Pauline taught Thérèse at the time of her first Communion, to keep score of acts of charity just as Thérèse had recorded how many times she repeated "Little Jesus, I love You."[24] But as Thérèse shed this manner of praying, she shed, too, any formula for charity. In her letters of the last seven years the traditional word "charity" appears only five times.[25] Yet these letters reveal 242 uses of the noun "Love" and 321 used of the verb "to love," generally directed to God, to Jesus.[26]

To clarify how Thérèse interpreted her vocation to "be Love" it helps to see clearly what it did not mean to her. Because she was firm and dealt directly with their moods, her novices, she said, found her "severe." "...(They) can say what they please," she wrote the last summer, "in the depths of their hearts they feel that I love them with a real love...I am prepared to lay down my life for them, but my affection

[23]B, p. 194.
[24]TE, p. 24, & GCI, p. 191, ft. 4.
[25]"Index Des Mots Principaux Des Lettres de Thérèse" in CG II, p. 1358.
[26]*Ibid,* pp. 1354 & 1355.

is so pure that I don't want them to know it...never have I
tried to attract their hearts to me..."[27] Love was not weakness, mere sweetness, or human attraction. Nor was it intimacy or blind loyalty to one's friends or family—she did not
confide in her sisters, and in the heated election of 1896
revealed not "the slightest animosity" towards Pauline's political foes.[28] In July of the final summer Thérèse refused
Pauline's request that she "say a few edifying and friendly
words" to Dr. de Cornière for whom Thérèse lacked respect.
"...this isn't my style..." Thérèse told Pauline. "Let Dr. de
Cornière think what he wants. I love only simplicity. I have a
horror for 'pretense.'..."[29] Love dictated neither fixed
manners nor guarding always against hurt feelings.

In Thérèse's milieu the summation of Christian Love was
what Jesus had termed the Second Great Commandment, so
commonly quoted as to have become a cliché: Love your
neighbor as yourself. Though it was virtually unquestioned,
Thérèse recognized a flaw in this formula:

"When the Lord commanded His people to love their
neighbor as themselves, He had not as yet come upon the
earth. Knowing the extent to which each one loved himself,
He was not able to ask of His creatures a greater love than
this for one's neighbor."[30] From her reading of the Old Testament Thérèse understood that when Jesus spoke these
words in response to a question he was quoting from the
book of Leviticus 19:18. This was the Old Law; it did not
sum up his final teaching, which was far more radical.
"...when Jesus gave his Apostles a new commandment,
HIS OWN COMMANDMENT, as He calls it later on, it is
no longer a question of loving one's neighbor as oneself but
of loving him as *He, Jesus, has loved him* ..."[31]

This meant laying down one's life, but not only in the

[27]C, p. 239.
[28]TE, p. 279.
[29]LA, p. 77. See also, LA, p. 71.
[30]C, p. 220.
[31]*Ibid.*

single act of death. Thérèse set out to feed the hungry and heal the sick as she found them there in the Carmel.

"We are surrounded," she told Céline, "by...souls in need, by weak souls and souls that are sick and oppressed ...share your substance with the poor...open up your house and part with your possessions. In other words, make a complete sacrifice of your rest and tranquility."[32] An often quoted example of Thérèse's love is the case of Sister St. Pierre, the irritable crippled nun whom Thérèse helped each night from the choir to the refectory.[33] This was a kind physical service, a patient act of charity which took place during Thérèse's early years in the Carmel. During the next several years Thérèse's understanding of love deepened, demanding far more of her. When she was a patient in the infirmary during the last summer Thérèse told Céline "souls should be treated with the same tender care" as were the sick sisters who were given "soft downy linens." "...Why is it that we forget this so frequently, and allow those about us to go on unnoticed in the endurance of sharp interior pain? Shouldn't the spiritual needs of the soul be attended to with the same...delicate care which we devote to...bodily needs?"[34] Thérèse lived among people who performed external acts in an effort to be charitable—prepared tidbits of food, gave little gifts, covered a sick sister with a soft blanket. But from her own experience she knew how few felt the obligation to try to heal the *interior* pain of a "soul in captivity,"[35] particularly an irritating one.

Thérèse's treatment of Sister Marie of St. Joseph whose "difficult and sick temperament exercised the patience of the community"[36] provides a little practical insight into how she treated these souls. No one wanted to work beside this petu-

[32]ME, p. 125.
[33]C, pp. 247-9.
[34]ME, 130-31.
[35]ME, pp. 126 & 131.
[36]DE, p. 862.

lant nun in the laundry room; Thérèse volunteered.[37] She worked there even after the initial vomiting of blood.[38] During Thérèse's final year alive she wrote Sister Marie of St. Joseph nine letters in which she joked and even adopted a private nickname for the unpopular laundress: the little boy. "Tomorrow," Thérèse wrote at the end of a letter designed to yank sister Marie out of a gloomy "combat", "we shall march arm in arm together!. . ."[39] As with Maurice Bellière, Thérèse took a strong personal interest in Sister Marie of St. Joseph, and worked to build her trust. "It is not her fault if she is so poorly gifted," Thérèse told her Sister Marie. "She is like an old clock that has to be rewound every quarter of an hour."[40]

". . .I understand, now," Thérèse wrote to the Prioress in her final copybook, "that charity consists in bearing with the faults of others, in not being surprised at their weakness, in being edified by the smallest acts of virtue we see them practice."[41] We know too little about the nun who ruled the Carmel laundry to explore Thérèse's response to her very deeply. Perhaps the relationship that most reveals what it cost Thérèse to "be love" to others was with her Prioress, the woman whom, years later, Pauline Martin denounced in a formal statement signed by five other nuns,[42] and whom Sister Marie of the Trinity called "the wolf."[43]

* * * * *

Mother Marie de Gonzague is a woman difficult for the modern eye to see; she steps out of the 19th century like a Dickens character. Devoted to the Carmelite order, her aris-

[37]LA, p. 95.

[38]ME, p. 213.

[39]Thérèse to Sister Marie of Saint Joseph, LT 194, 8-17 September, 1897, CG II, p. 886.

[40]TE, p. 94.

[41]C, p. 220.

[42]*Summarium,* 1916, 1920. Archives of the Carmel of Lisieux.

[43]TE, p. 232.

tocratic bearing, conversational skill and appealing manner masked a quite human failing: she never detached herself from the aristocratic status to which she was born. For all but three of the nine and a half years Thérèse spent in the cloister, Mother Marie de Gonzague held nearly absolute authority over her.

"I know that she loved me very much," Thérèse wrote to Pauline in her copybook, "and said everything good about me that was possible, nevertheless, God permitted that she was VERY SEVERE, *without her even being aware of it*. I was unable to meet her without having to kiss the floor..."[44]

Mother Marie de Gonzague's harshness to Thérèse as a young novice grew out of an energetic devotion to the ascetic ideal. To her credit, she recognized Thérèse's "calibre." Given her assumptions, she was not persecuting Thérèse but training her to the heights of perfection. Thérèse later wrote to the Prioress her appreciation "for not sparing me".[45]

The Prioress's more serious defect was the pitfall of those in absolute power: identifying one's own prejudices and whims with the good of the community. Even as a young nun Thérèse recognized this defect. From time to time Mother Marie de Gonzague welcomed her aristocratic sister and her grandchildren for overnight visits; the grandchildren played in the superior's parlor, and the Carmelites became servants.[46] Summoned one evening during the Grand Silence to prepare a lamp for yet another visit of the Prioress's noble sister, Thérèse fought a "violent" internal struggle against authority.[47]

More serious and personal trials were to come. The 1896 elections for Prioress were scheduled within weeks of the date when Céline Martin, the fourth of the Martin sisters to enter the monastery, was due to make her profession. The

[44]A, p. 150.

[45]C, p. 206.

[46]*Summarium*, p. 172.

[47]LA, p. 90.

obvious contenders: Pauline Martin, the current Prioress, and Mother Marie de Gonzague, then Mistress of Novices. Anticipating victory, Mother Marie de Gonzague used her current position to try to block Céline's profession until after the election.[48]

That a human motivation might block her sister's solemn vows provoked the single reported case of Thérèse's "losing a little of that calm" while in the convent. The witness, Sister Aimée of Jesus of the faction hostile to the "Martin clan," testified that the subject of Céline's profession came up one day while she worked with Thérèse in the laundry room:

"Mother Marie de Gonzague has a perfect right to try Sister Geneviève (Céline), why does it surprise you?" said Sister Aimèe of Jesus. Thérèse responded "with emotion:"

"What upsets me is a type of trial which they have no right to use."[49] Mother Marie de Gonzague won the election but lost the battle to delay Céline's profession. The episode deepened the cleavage between her and the Martin faction. It seems that Mother Marie de Gonzague had hoped not only to be elected but to soundly rout Pauline on the first ballot. She did defeat Pauline, but only on the seventh ballot and she felt the humiliation bitterly.[50]

The wounds did not heal quickly. They continued to fester even three months later at the celebration honoring Mother Marie de Gonzague on her feast day. "For this feast, it was necessary to thrust all uppermost feelings underneath," Marie testified.[51] Apparently some did not succeed. In her continuing humiliation the 62 year old head of the community turned now to the only nun in the convent she completely trusted[52]: the 23 year old Thérèse. Mother Marie de Gonzague wept; in a tantrum she threatened to leave the

[48]"Note Sur Mere Marie de Gonzague et la Profession de Soeur Geneviève," CG II, pp. 1181-1185.

[49]*Ibid*, p. 1183.

[50]CGII, p. 844. and 848.

[51]GC II, pp. 858.

[52]DE, p. 25, ft. 15.

convent.[53] Complicating Thérèse's natural reactions, this outburst occurred two and a half months after she first vomited blood and sank into inner darkness. The Prioress took little note of Thérèse's physical problem at this point, and was unaware of her inner torment. In spite of her own struggles, Thérèse contained her feelings in order to soothe the wounded pride of the idol who had failed.

Thérèse wrote her a long, kind letter in the form of a legend: as advocate of Mother Marie de Gonzague's point of view Thérèse, the lamb, questions the Lord on her behalf. The lamb asks the Lord why, if he were determined to put the crook back in the Shepherdess' hands, "why not have done it after the *first* ballot?"

Because, he answers, "I *love* your Shepherdess." In a long dialogue filled with tenderness, he explains that this was her chosen trial.

"Seeing its Shepherdess weep," Thérèse writes, "the poor little creature was afflicted and sought in vain in its very small heart the way to console her whom it loved *more than itself*...."[54] For Thérèse this phrase was quite literally true. There were no conditions on her love, as there were no conditions on Christ's love.

The election for Prioress in 1896 had a very significant personal impact on Thérèse: Mother Marie de Gonzague and not Pauline would have authority over her long and painful final illness. Sister Marie of the Trinity reports that after the initial vomiting of blood in April of 1896 Thérèse "grew steadily worse... Unknown to her I went to Mother Gonzague and asked her to let Sister Thérèse stay in bed during Matins, but she repulsed me, saying: 'I've never seen young people take such care of their health as you do. There was a time when nobody would be absent from Matins. If Sister Thérèse cannot manage it any more, let her come and tell me so herself.'...."[55]

[53]CG II, p. 858.
[54]Thérèse to Mother de Gonzague, LT 190, June 29, 1896, p. 858.
[55]TE, p. 243.

Because Mother Marie de Gonzague was Prioress, Thérèse was tended in her long final illness not by her relative by
marriage, Dr. Francis La Néele, but by the regular physician
to the Carmel in whom the Prioress had great confidence,
Dr. de Cornière. While TB patients at sanitaria took rest
cures, he used techniques such as the *points de feu,* blistering
the back with hot needles. During one session the Prioress
and the Doctor chatted, according to Céline, "about the
most trivial things." Thérèse then went to her room to lie on
a straw mattress on her wooden bed.[56] In late August when
tuberculosis invaded Thérèse's intestines and she was tempted to suicide, Dr. de Cornière was on vacation. For a week
Mother Marie de Gonzague refused to summon Dr. La
Néele.[57] When he finally was contacted and saw Thérèse's
condition, Dr. La Néele "said very hard things to the Prioress," reducing her to tears.[58] In September the Prioress
refused permission for injections of morphine during the
final tormented weeks. Céline's testimony makes clear that
this decision came not out of cruelty but from a fixed idea:
"...sedatives were prohibited as a disgrace..."[59]

Truly it was not out of cruelty: the previous Lent Mother
Marie de Gonzague had ordered Thérèse to take a piece of
chocolate each day;[60] during the winter she gave her a *chauf-
ferette,* a grill with hot coals to warm the feet and sandals.[61]
In fact, Mother Marie de Gonzague held Thérèse in such
high regard that she told Sister Marie of the Trinity several
times,

"If a prioress were to be chosen from the whole community, I wouldn't hesitate to choose Sister Thérèse, in spite of
her youth. She is perfect in everything; her only drawback is
the presence of her three sisters."[62]

[56]ME, p. 214.
[57]TE, p. 92.
[58]DE, p. 177.
[59]DE, 555.
[60]DE, p. 31, ft. 53.
[61]ME, p. 73.
[62]TE, p. 253.

Thérèse's tenderness to this woman, based both on under-standing and ignoring her flaws, survived even the ordeal of tuberculosis. Her farewell letter to Father Roulland ends,

"*Au revoir,* my Brother, pray very much for your sister, pray *for Our Mother,* whose sensitive mother's heart cannot easily consent to my leaving. I count on you to console her."[63] Mother Marie de Gonzague's refusal to summon a doctor during the agonizing last week of August angered the Martin sisters, but not Thérèse.[64] As we have seen, her dying "look," so coveted by Céline, went to the Prioress.[65]

The command to love her neighbor "as he, Jesus, had loved him" was a command to love Mother Marie de Gon-zague, even while the Prioress's decisions left Thérèse in torment. Her love was not based as pictures and statues might suggest, on a *naive* sweetness that sees no evil. Thé-rèse's love was rooted in her clear insight into people. This may lead some to retreat into the notion that her sanctity explains her behavior, as if her sanctity were there from the start like a finished piece of embroidery. In this view an ordinary person could not give love to those whom Thérèse did. Her relationship with Mother Marie de Gonzague becomes The Villain versus The Saint. But Thérèse did not view her sisters as villains, only flawed human beings, and she wrestled with her own feelings as any normal human being does.[66] "Violent" as those feelings sometimes were in her early years in the Carmel, Thérèse recognized that love was Jesus' *command.* Reasoning that he does not "com-mand the impossible," she found a solution:

"...You know very well that never would I be able to love my Sisters as You love them, unless *You,* O my Jesus, *loved them in me...*"[67] That her ability to love even rigid, judg-mental and tyrannizing souls sprang from a deeper well than

[63]Thérèse to P. Roulland, LT, p. 254, July 14, 1897, CGII., p. 1030.

[64]TE, p. 92.

[65]LA, p. 229.

[66]C, p. 225.

[67]C, p. 221.

herself is clear from her prayer for her novices and her two spiritual brothers:

> Your love has gone before me, and it has grown within me, and now it is an abyss whose depths I cannot fathom. Love attracts love, and, my Jesus, my love leaps toward Yours...For me to love You as You love me, I would have to borrow Your own Love...O my Jesus, it is perhaps an illusion but it seems to me that You cannot fill a soul with more love than the love with which you have filled mine; it is for this reason that I dare to ask You *"to love those whom you have given me with the love with which you loved me."*[68]

As a "little soul" stripped of any significant role in human terms, Thérèse was the ideal conduit of this message to a world shackled to fixed identities. Shedding all efforts to bolster a humanly molded self left her free for the act of loving, continuously renewed. Thérèse ends her offering of herself to God's love by saying she wants to renew the offering "at each beat of my heart...an infinite number of times." Her love was neither static nor directed solely to God. She also renewed the act of loving from minute to minute with those around her: with Sister Marie of St. Joseph in the laundry room, with Mother Marie de Gonzague at her bedside.

[68]C, p. 256.

X

The Language of Nature

What are the roots that clutch, what branches grow
Out of this stony rubbish? Son of man
You cannot say, or guess, for you know only
A heap of broken images...[1]
T.S. Eliot, *The Wasteland*, 1922

My folly consists in begging the eagles, my brothers,
to obtain for me the favor of flying towards the Sun of
Love with the *Divine Eagle's own wings!*[2]
Thérèse Martin, 1896

The year before Thérèse died William Butler Yeats sat in a French theater 100 miles from the Carmel of Lisieux and watched a brutal play called *Ubi Roi*, a harbinger of the harsh abstraction of the modern era.

"... The players are supposed to be dolls, toys, marionettes, and now they are all hopping like wooden frogs..." he wrote in his journal. "The chief personage, who is some kind of King, carries for sceptre a brush of the kind that we

---

[1] T.S. Eliot, *The Wasteland* in Alexander W. Allison *et at, Norton* Anthology of Poetry, (New York, 1975), p. 514.

[2] B. p. 200.

use to clean a closet. . . I am very sad. . .after our own verse, after all our subtle colour and nervous rhythm, after the faint mixed tints of Condor, what more is possible? After us the Savage God."[3] Much of the traditional form and sentimental language of the past was outmoded; unless a way were found to convey concretely the deeper life of the spirit the Savage God would reign alone.

Yeats wrote those sad lines as a poet. Those committed to the ancient message of the Church faced the same challenge. Over much of the Church's imagery lay a coating of sentimentality abhorrent to the sons and daughters of the middle class breaking old molds with their newly acquired education and craving to experience life. Faced with Yeats' conflict, few were able to sift through the pile of holy sayings, prayers, pious books and pictures repeated and accumulated over centuries. How did one begin to evaluate words and practices held sacred by thousands of good believing men and women? If the life of the spirit were to reach those living on the brink of the world of the Savage God, the gloss of false mystery had to be scraped from the truly sacred. One had to meditate on the symbols of the past in order to recognize the symbols of the present, then select elements of language stripped of the fine shadings and embellishments, stripped of the stale and static words so distant from the ordinary person's way of seeing and distant too from the brutal life of some, the empty life of others. That language must speak clearly and dig down deep enough to capture the real craving, the real conflict and longings of those cut adrift.

In 1896, two months before Thérèse experienced her Christmas Eve conversion at age 13 in Lisieux, the Viscomte Charles de Foucauld, back in Paris to write a book after charting the land of Morocco, entered a confessional and told the priest:

"Monsieur l'Abbé, I have no faith. I come to ask for

---

[3]W.B. Yeats, *The Autobiography of W.B. Yeats,* (N.Y.: Macmillan, 1953), p. 210. I am indebted to John Wain for this insight. He treats the question thoroughly in "Poetry," in *The Twentieth Century Mind I: 1900-1918,* (London: Oxford U. Press, 1972), pp. 260-411.

instruction."[4] The stark power of the desert Arabs stopping five times a day to pray convinced Charles de Foucauld of his own emptiness. He entered the strictest order he could find: the Trappists. Unsatisfied, he left France for the most solitary and poorest monastery he could find: at Akbes, Syria. Still he was discontent. The year that Thérèse Martin died Charles de Foucauld left the Trappists on a quest. Desiring to know Jesus more concretely, he went to the one spot on earth where he would find both the solitude he craved and more tangible contact with Jesus' life. He arrived in Nazareth 6 months before Thérèse died. In a wooden tool shed built against the side of the Poor Clares' convent Charles de Foucauld lived in silence and solitude, received and contemplated the Eucharist, and worked as a gardener and handyman.

Charles loved John of the Cross and practiced an extreme form of detachment and self-effacement. To approach close to the actual, not the imagined, life of Jesus with the Gospels as his guide, Charles wrote out Jesus' story in little texts appropriate to each day of the year. His text for December 21:

"The Blessed Virgin and Saint Joseph left Nazareth this morning to go to Bethlehem. They crossed the plain of Esdraelon and probably found food and shelter this night somewhere near Engannim towards Jenin or Zababda..."[5] The simple description echoes the comment Thérèse made to Pauline in August, 1897. "For a sermon on the Blessed Virgin to please me... I must see her real life, not her imagined life. I'm sure that her real life was very simple."[6] Nine months after Thérèse died Charles wrote from Nazareth to a fellow Trappist, cautioning him to be content to be as a child:

---

[4]Charles de Foucauld, *Meditations of a Hermit*, trans. Charlotte Balfour. (New York: Orbis Books, 1981,), p. xviii.

[5]*Ibid.* p. ix.

[6]LA, p. 161.

...This life was enough for him, the Son of God, for many years. Let it be enough for you...it is as though you were five years old and were learning to read, like a child, and humbly and obediently do all you are told, just as Jesus at five years old did all that his parents told him.

Later he will take you to the desert...from there to Gethsamane...then to Calvary...[7]

Charles de Foucauld wrote these lines before Thérèse's writings were published. He knew nothing about her.

In 1877, the year that Thérèse's mother died and the Martin family moved to Lisieux, Gerard Manley Hopkins was ordained a priest on the other side of the English Channel. Father Hopkins, too, had experienced a conversion. Before entering the priesthood he had written some poetry but, determined to contain his own ego, he burned his early poems.

When a group of German nuns drowned in England in 1875 Hopkins's superior suggested that he write again; he continued to write poetry until he died, the year Thérèse entered the Carmel. Valuing his faith more than his art, like Thérèse, he published almost nothing in his lifetime. After his poetry finally appeared in 1918 it startled the literary more than the religious world. Intellectuals cynical in the wake of World War I read compact, blunt language foreign to the cultivated ear, common Old English and Welsh and Irish rhythms of speech. It was an odd language for a Classics scholar and Jesuit priest who daily prayed the Mass and Divine Office in Latin. But Hopkins had searched for a form and a language to express the central vision of his life—his personal, silent God revealed concretely through the things of the earth. Latin, abstract and remote from the living reality all about him, and much of the cultivated language derived from it, failed to convey the mystery of the living God as did the living speech of the people, simple, concrete images, and the blunt old rhythms that joined the two:

[7]Charles de Foucauld, p. 138.

> The world is charged with the grandeur of God.
> It will flame out, like shining from shook foil;
> It gathers to a greatness, like the ooze of oil
> Crushed. Why do men then now not reck his rod?[8]

Unlike Thérèse, Father Hopkins was a well-trained and broadly read scholar, a student of old languages that she would like to have studied, a disciplined and original poet. This distinction, which would appear so significant in their own day, makes all the more remarkable the elements of style and insight they shared. Father Hopkins' "...does Thou touch me afresh? Over again I feel thy finger and find thee," is startlingly distinct from the prayers of the day, but springs from the same insight as Thérèse's "hiding my face in his hair."[9]

Father Hopkins labored quietly for years over exact language. Charles de Foucauld after leaving Nazareth lived alone in the mountains of Algeria with only the Eucharist and any traveller who needed food or lodging, while translating the tribal poetry of the Tuaregs into French. Like Thérèse, each of these men lived a hidden life, shut off from the dizzying change of their day. Each meditated to grasp the essentials of the tradition they loved from within, but turned away from the familiar formal language to simple, tangible words of ordinary speech to try to convey the mystery.

In an echo of World War I, in 1916 Charles de Foucauld, living alone in Tamanrasset in the Algerian Hoggar, was dragged outside and murdered. When friends found him dead, knowing that the center of his life was the Eucharist they searched about his hermitage for the consecrated Host. They found the Host, but not in a golden tabernacle. Charles had hidden it in the sand.

*   *   *   *   *

When at age 14 Thérèse awakened from the years of self-absorption following her mother's death to resume her

---

[8]G.M. Hopkins, *God's Grandeur* in Allison *et al,* p. 424.
[9]C, p. 238.

"childhood character" she discovered Thomas à Kempis. In his third book (four books comprise *The Imitation of Christ)* Thomas wrote a warm and deeply personal dialogue between The Disciple and Christ, drawing on sources not very familiar to French Catholic households. He selected short passages, sometimes just a phrase, from both the Old and the New Testaments, weaving these words into the imaginary dialogue. The theme throughout is the strict renouncing of the world, material things, the self, with a firm and loving voice summoning the Disciple to a deeper life. Thomas à Kempis selected that part of the Judeo-Christian literary tradition that brims with love, compassion and human weakness. In his dialogue he mingles the *Psalms*, the *Song of Songs*, *Job*, *Sirach*, *Isaiah*, *Jeremiah*, St. Paul, and the words of Jesus:

> The Disciple:
>
> O Lord, You thunder your judgments overhead and all my bones shudder in fear and trembling. *My soul is strangely terrified,* (Job 37:1-2) I stand frozen in amazement and believe that *the heavens themselves are not pure in Your sight.*[10] (Job 15:15)
>
> When will I be with You *in the kingdom you have prepared from all eternity for those who love You?* (Matthew 25:34) I am but a poor abandoned exile in a hostile land...[11]

Blending phrases from two different books of the Bible, Thomas placed them in Jesus' mouth:

> *Because your soul was precious in My sight* (1 Samuel 26:21) *I turned my eye toward you and saved you* (Ezekiel 20:17) I preserved you because I wanted you to feel My Love...[12]

---

[10]IC, p. 134. All biblical references are those cited in Joseph Tylenda's translation of *The Imitation of Christ.*

[11]IC, p. 194.

[12]IC, p. 134.

Thomas even manages to weave together the words of St. Paul with the poetry of the psalms in one seamless thought:

> In You I glory and *exult all the day long.* (Psalm 89:16)
> *But as for myself I boast in nothing except my weakness.*
> (2 Cor. 12:5)[13]

Thérèse did not merely *read* the passages that she loved, she absorbed them. "I knew almost all the chapters of my beloved *Imitation* by heart."[14] Like Thomas à Kempis, Thérèse too wove together the scriptures and her own insights in a conversation with The Lord. A literal translation of Deuteronomy 32:11 reads:

> As the eagle stirs up its nest
> Over its young it hovers,
> It spreads out its wings
> Takes it, (and) bears it on its wings.[15]

Thérèse writes: "Jesus, I am too little to perform great actions, and my own *folly* is this: to trust that your Love will accept me as a victim. My *folly* consists in begging the eagles, my brothers, to obtain for me the favor of flying towards the sun of Love with the *Divine Eagle's own wings!*"[16]

Thérèse, like Charles de Foucauld, read the poetry of John of the Cross. As we have seen, John writes of spiritual love through the most concrete of sensual imagery:

> And then we will go on
> to the high caverns in the rock
> which are so well concealed;

---

[13]IC, p. 181.

[14]A, p. 102.

[15]Jay Green (ed. & trans.). *The Interlinear Hebrew/Greek/English Bible,* Vol. One, (Wilmington, Delaware, 1976), p. 549.

[16]B, p. 200.

There we shall enter
And taste the fresh juice of the pomegranates.[17]

In John of the Cross's poetry there are nightingales, river banks, turtledoves, foxes, roses, pines, balsam and spiced wine. He expresses the individual soul's relationship to God through the most human details:

You considered
That one hair fluttering at my neck;
You gazed at it upon my neck
And it captivated You;
And one of my eyes wounded You.[18]

Except for a few of the French Romantic poets, the *Psalms, The Song of Songs,* and John of the Cross, were Thérèse's essential exposures to poetry. She wrote her first poem in 1893. In the next four and a half years before her death she produced fifty-four completed poems and three fragments.[19] She used rhyme, which does not translate well. This excerpt from a fifty-five stanza poem lacks the density and control of John of the Cross's poetry but it comes from a twenty-two year old completely untrained, with very little time for writing.

. . .
I love to gather heather
Running along the light moss.
Fluttering among the fern
The butterflies reflect pure
    Azure.
. . .

The grass is murdered under my step
The flower withers in my hands
Jesus, I want to run in your meadow

---

[17]CWJC, *The Spiritual Canticle,* p. 414.
[18]*Ibid.*
[19]All published in *Poésies* (Editions du Cerf et Desclee de Brouwer, 1979).

Where no mark is left
By my step.[20]

As she found the familiar formulas of human language
inadequate to explain her "inner darkness,"[21] Thérèse found
human language insufficient to express other spiritual experiences as well. In a conversation with Pauline during her
final summer Thérèse made clear that she intentionally
employed images to convey a deeper level of reality. They
were speaking about the Holy Innocents, the infants under
the age of two whom Herod slaughtered at the time of
Christ's birth. These infants had slipped into the culture of
sentimentality as "the children of heaven." Pauline reports:
"The Holy Innocents, she said, are not the children of
Heaven; they only have the indefinable charms of childhood.
They are pictured as children, because we have need of
images to understand invisible things."[22]

To use fresh images confidently Thérèse had first to purge
herself of some images of the world to which she was born
which had lost their power in her day; some conveyed more

[20]"Le Cantique de Céline," stanzas 26 and 33, in *Poésies*, pp. 107 & 108.
J'amais à cueillir la bruyère
Courant sur la mousse légère
Je prenais voltigeant sur la fougère
Les papillons au reflet pur
    D'azure.
. . .
Sous mes pas l'herbe s'est meurtrie!
La fleur en mes mains s'est flétrie! Jésus, je veux couris en ta prairie
Sure elle ne marqueront pas
    Mes pas. . .
Some translations distort the tone of Thérèse's writing. In a 1926 edition of her
autobiography, for example, in order to preserve rhyme the above stanza is
translated:
The grass is withered in its bed
The flowers within my hands are dead
Would that my weary feet, Jesus! might tread
Thy heavenly Fields, and I might be
    With Thee!
From Thomas N. Taylor, *Saint Thérèse of Lisieux, The Little Flower of Jesus*
(P.J.Kenedy & Sons: N.Y., 1926), p. 380.
[21]C, p. 212.
[22]DE, p. 424. (Quoted from Apostolic Process, 630, p. 259.)

superstition than true mystery. The *Grimm's Fairy Tales* of French children were the *Fables of La Fontaine.* In Pauline Martin's copy which Thérèse read as a child, a famous illustration by de Staal pictured Death as a skeleton in a feathered hat. According to Céline, Thérèse was "not able to endure this image."[23] During Thérèse's final summer when Pauline was frightened by her coming death Thérèse told her, "It's not 'death' that will come in search of me, it's God. Death isn't some phantom, some horrible spectre as it is represented in pictures. It is said in the catechism that 'death is the separation of the soul from the body,' and that is all it is."[24]

That certain symbols had seeped into the consciousness of many religious people of his day deflecting them from a deeper reality had disturbed Thomas à Kempis:

> Many people travel to different places to pay homage to the relics of the saints, and they stand in amazement when they see the splendid shrines, and are in awe when they hear narrated the story of the saints' lives and their remarkable deeds, or again, when they kiss the bones wrapped in silk and encased in gold. But You, my God...are here present before me on this altar![25]

Preserved bodies continued to hold great appeal in the 19th century. In Dostoyevsky's *The Brothers Karamazov,* the faithful more or less expected that the body of a holy person would be preserved.

On her pilgrimage to Rome Thérèse had seen preserved bodies and parts of bodies of saints. A member of the pilgrimage describes the corpse of Saint Catherine of Bologna:

> We were admitted to venerate the corpse of the saint and to kiss her feet and her hands. The Blessed One is seated in an armchair... Her corpse is admirably preserved, the

[23]DE, p. 415. Félix LeMaistre, *Fables,* (Garnier Frères: Paris, MDCCCLXIX).
[24]LA, p . 41.
[25]IC, p. 230.

limbs are flexible, the blood tinged sweat which oozed
when they lifted it out of the tomb, 18 days after her death
to put her in the place which she occupies without other
support, has stayed quite liquid. . . [26]

Another pilgrim on that same trip recorded: "her face and
her hands are blackened by time."[27]

Thérèse explicitly told her sisters that she had no desire to
be venerated in this way after she died. "I would rather be
reduced to ashes than to be preserved like St. Catherine of
Bologna. I know only St. Crispino who came forth from the
tomb with honor,"[28] Thérèse quipped to Pauline the day she
was carried down to the infirmary where she would die.
Marie reports the same: "We said to her, my sisters and I,
how happy we would be if her corpse were preserved, and
she answered, 'You will not find me anything but a little
skeleton. . .'"[29]

For Thérèse this type of sign was too dramatic, coupled
with the old heroic notion of the saint. It would set her apart
as *other* than the ordinary people she hoped would imitate
her way. ". . . we knew," Pauline later wrote, "she would not
be preserved after death."[30] She died on Thursday, September 30th. Like Father Zossima, her body soon began to
decay:

"After she was dead she preserved a sweet smile," Pauline
testified in 1910. "She looked ravishingly beautiful. As is the
custom in Carmel, she was laid out in the choir, by the grille.
By Sunday evening, 3 October, there were some signs of
decomposition, and the coffin was closed. She was buried on
4 October at the Lisieux cemetery, without anything out of
the ordinary happening."[31]

[26]Quoted in DE, pp. 458-9.

[27]*Ibid.*

[28]LA, p. 80.

[29]DE, p. 458. (Quoted from Apostolic Process, pp. 2343).

[30]LA, p. 128.

[31]TE, p. 69.

Thérèse turned instead to the living symbols of nature, the best known of which was flowers, a natural choice for one who lived on a farm during most of her first 15 months and was wheeled in a wheelbarrow into the fields where she picked wildflowers. Yet in a country where flowers filled the windowboxes and courtyards, flowers were generally overlooked as a symbol of life and death. The faithful turned instead to traditional symbols connected with the saints. Mother Marie of the Angels, Thérèse's Novice Mistress, testified:

"A feature of her piety that struck me particularly, because I had never heard it spoken of in Carmel or in the lives of the saints, was the role she attributed to flowers...Late on a summer's evening, in the time of silence...she would strew flowers round the base of the Calvary in the cloister garth..."[32]

Unfortunately, flowers were easily sentimentalized, distorting the distinctly realistic vision of Thérèse. Sentiment, as Flannery O'Connor has pointed out, is a distortion stemming from an overly simplified view of life. Thérèse's sisters *were* sentimental, an understandable feeling in the context of her terrible death.

Four months before she died Thérèse wrote a poem in which she used an unpetaled rose as the image of herself.

Jesus, when I see you, held up by your Mother,
    Quit her arms
To try, trembling, on our sad earth
    Your first steps
Before you I would like *to unpetal a rose*
    In its freshness
That your small foot might gently rest
    On a flower!

This unpetaled rose is the true image
    Divine Child

[32]TE, p. 208.

> Of the heart that wants to sacrifice itself completely
> At each instant...[33]

In her view Jesus had "...no need of our works but only of our *love*..."[34] The act of strewing "...these fragile, worthless petals, these songs of love from the littlest of hearts..."[35] was the metaphor for her life.

But this act was frozen into an idealized image in art. Over the next 30 years Céline painted her dead sister's portrait time after time. As the years added distance from the real Thérèse, as she was spoken of more widely as a saint, Céline's paintings became less real, more ethereal. Her famous portrait of Thérèse cradling a bouquet of roses glowed like a polished halo.[36] The image is quite different from Thérèse's own "unpetaled rose." It was Céline's awkward effort to distill Thérèse's symbol into art and to capture in a "heavenly" manner[37] the symbolism behind the sight that seared into the Martin sisters' memories: their 24 year old little sister lying in the hot infirmary dying of tuberculosis, sometimes sweating so that the sheets were soaked through,[38]

---

[33]"Une Rose effeuillée." *Poésies*, p. 229.

Jésus, quand je te vois soutenu par ta Mère
  Quitter ses bras
Essayer en tremblant sur notre triste terre
  Tes premiers pas
Devant toi je voudrais effeuiller une rose
  En sa fraîcheur
Pour que ton petit pied bien doucement repose
  Sur une fleur!

Cette rose effeuillée, c'est la fidèle image
  Divine Enfant
Du Coeur qui veut pou toi s'immoler sans partage
  A chaque instant...

[34]B, p. 189.

[35]C, p. 197.

[36]An excellent account of Céline's paintings and retouching of Thérèse's photographs appears in Peter-Thomas Rohrback, O.C.D., *Photo Album of Saint Thérèse of Lisieux*, (N.Y., 1962).

[37]*Ibid*, p. 40. The word appears in Céline's instructions to another artist.

[38]Pauline to the Guérin's, Aug. 5, 1897, LA, p. 286.

at other times in such pain that she could not bear their touch,[39] but delighting in the fresh flowers that were brought to her. And flowers *were* brought to her: violets, roses, dahlias, and, of course, wild cornflowers.[40] The wildflowers might have served as a more appropriate symbol of Thérèse, who told Pauline at the beginning of her copybook of memories: "...if all flowers wanted to be roses, nature would lose her springtime beauty and the fields would no longer be decked out with little wild flowers...He willed to create great souls comparable to lillies and roses, but He has created smaller ones and these must be content to be daisies or violets..."[41]

Thérèse fled the clutter of French middle class life with its *objets d'art,* matching outfits, and fine food and wine, for the stark cloister with rhythmic chanting, the wood, the sand-glass, the hemp sandals, the straw mattress, the brown wool robe, crockery dishes and stone—everywhere was stone. In a setting cleansed of the artificial, the merely ornamental or convenient, she strewed flowers. A colorful relief against the wood and the stone, flowers decorated the chapel which housed the single most powerful living symbol of the entire tradition: The Eucharist. Thérèse absorbed the living symbol of flowers as she absorbed the living language of the past, not out of mere sentiment, but only to put her in closer touch with a deeper reality. She was not drawn to carefully sculpted arrangements of hot-house flowers: she asked explicitly that money be spent to help black babies in Africa rather than to buy flowers for her coffin.[42] "After my death," she told Pauline, "I don't want to be surrounded with wreaths of flowers as Mother Geneviève was."[43]

We are now brought full circle, back where we started: the 13 year old Thérèse's withdrawal into Pauline's old attic

---

[39]LA, p. 189.

[40]TE, p. 96, LA, pp. 189, 190, 192.

[41]A, p. 14.

[42]LA, p. 47.

[43]*Ibid.*

room "...a real bazaar, an assemblage of pious objects and curiosities, a garden and an aviary."[44] In that room Thérèse "...cultivated pots of flowers (the rarest I could find)..." and in front of the statue of the blessed Virgin sat "...vases always filled with natural flowers..."[45] Thérèse stressed that the flowers were natural. When she no longer found her security in possessions, Thérèse carried with her into the Carmel the memory of the natural things she had selected to surround her in the attic room: the birds, the plants, the flowers. The images of nature flowed into her written memories, her letters, her poems: eagles, doves, the star, the sun, fire, snow, the grain of sand, the desert, birds, plants, flowers. To touch the images that touched Thérèse one need not travel on a pilgrimage to a remote place.

* * * * *

Though indifferent to and cut off from the artistic currents of her day, during her final summer alive Thérèse recognized the importance of her writing. She warned Pauline to take care lest human motivations block its publication. "After my death you mustn't speak to anyone about my manuscript before it is published; you must speak about it only to Mother Prioress..."[46] It was far more important that even Pauline had guessed. Only through Thérèse's writing did Pauline first recognize that her sister embodied the deep truths of their tradition.

Though her poetic skill was never trained, never had time to fully develop, some essential elements in Thérèse's writing prefigured the strong current of modern symbolism which shed the sentiment and absorption with the "self" of the Romantics, and shed abstract language for the concrete language of ordinary people, to explore the deeply imbedded images that reflected ancient meaning. Her perception was what Yeats groped toward in 1896 as he tried to slip out

[44]A, p. 90.
[45]*Ibid.*
[46]LA, p. 126.

from under the debris while clinging to the deep spiritual roots.

Twenty five years after Thérèse died T.S. Eliot's poem *The Wasteland,* was published. In this poem Eliot captured the mood of post-World War I Europe, its old forms shattered, its new habits empty and self-centered:

> ...what branches grow
> Out of this stony rubbish? Son of man
> You cannot say, or guess, for you know only
> a heap of broken images...[47]

Eliot was no poet of despair, no worshipper of the Savage God. He voiced the desolate cry of modern people facing a landscape of decay. *The Wasteland* is about the old legend of The Grail, the symbol of hopeful seeking of life's elusive meaning. Beneath the "heap of broken images" remained the stirrings of the life of the spirit. But Eliot's vision did not end with "The Wasteland." In "Ash Wednesday," a poem published after he accepted Christianity, he resurrected images and phrases that also hark back to ancient roots, but this time conveying hope. A quick glance at the following words might suggest that they were gleaned from Thérèse's memories and letters: rose, blessed face, tree, the rock, redeem, bird, exile, silence, desert, sand, solitude, surrender, darkness, eagle, wings. The words are all from T.S. Eliot's "Ash Wednesday."

Eliot, the great symbolist poet of the modern era who drew on the deepest of subconscious symbols from the past, after years of reflecting on ancient myths and texts, selected independently many of the same images that had flowed spontaneously from the young, untrained Thérèse. Her images were as simple and divested of the artificial as her brown woolen habit and crockery dish. They reflected, in fact, Jesus' own choice of simple images and symbols to express a deeper reality: water, seeds, yeast, trees, a child, common wine, bread.

---

[47]Eliot, in *Norton Anthology of Poetry,* p. 514.

Thérèse's letter to her sister Marie in September, 1896, begins with this caution: "...I am going to stammer some words even though I feel it is quite impossible for the human tongue to express things which the human heart can hardly understand."[48] She was speaking honestly, not modestly. We would do well to recall her caution, and Céline's mistake, when we see her words chiseled into stone beneath a haloed statue or baked in a rose hue at the feet of a stained glass saint. Thérèse speaks in a clear human voice to an anxious world "groping for its God;" but to hear that voice clearly we must listen to her own stammerings.

---

[48] B, p. 187.

A Note on Sources

When the first scholar to probe beneath the editions of *Histoire d'une Ame (Story of a Soul)* published with the blessing of Thérèse's sisters entered the Carmel Archives in 1945 he found Thérèse's original manuscripts in a shocking state. In correcting Thérèse's grammar and spelling, in rounding off into proper conventional phrases her blunt style, Pauline had extensively edited, and altered, Thérèse's writing. Many flowery phrases that people had come to know as Thérèse's words were, in fact, Pauline's. Céline assisted with scissors and a scraper, literally cutting and scraping away passages that seemed to reveal unnecessary details of family life or were merely unsaintly.

With Pauline's permission, but after her death, in 1956 a completely reliable facsimile copy of Thérèse's major autobiographical writings was published as the *manuscrits autobiographiques*. It included the childhood memories she had written for Pauline in 1895 (Manuscript A), a letter she wrote to Marie in 1896 (Manuscript B), and the spiritual insights she wrote for Mother Marie de Gonzague in 1897 (Manuscript C). The *manuscrits autobiographiques* was, indeed, precise; but lacking punctuation and Pauline's familiar headings and divisions into chapters it was a stark manuscript. In 1972 a new edition of *Histoire d'Une Âme* was published, incorporating Thérèse's actual words from the facsimile of her writings published in *manuscrits autobiographiques* with the sectional divisions familiar to readers. Father John Clarke's 1975 English translation, *Story of a Soul,* is a precise rendering of the 1972 French edition.

Father Clarke has translated other new sources as well. In his Introduction to *General Correspondence I,* he recounts the colorful story of various efforts to unveil the accurate and complete correspondence of St. Thérèse. Cooperation between scholars and the Carmel of Lisieux has resulted in the publication of the unabridged correspondence including letters written to Thérèse. Beginning with her first note written at four years of age every letter preserved is now in print, with extensive annotation, in the two volume *Correspondance Générale.* Volume I of the *Correspondance Générale* is in English, Volume II has been translated in preparation for publication.

Other major sources published within the last 15 years, and upon which I have also relied heavily, include: *St. Thérèse of Lisieux by those who knew her,* first hand testimony from her relatives and nuns who lived with her in the Carmel given at the Beatification Process only 13 years after she died; *Derniers Entretiens avec ses Soeurs,* a detailed, daily, sometimes hourly, account of her final illness and medical care, charts detailing the Carmel setting, schedule and practices, and Thérèse's conversations with Pauline (and others) over the final months of her life, annotated with explanations of the context of many of Thérèse's comments; *St. Thérèse of Lisieux, Her Last Conversations,* John Clarke's translation into English of the core of *Derniers Entretiens; La Bible avec Thérèse de Lisieux,* a compilation of the vast number of biblical references appearing in her writings; and *Poésies,* an integral edition of Thérèse's poems appearing only in 1979, a welcome addition to the sources, especially to those familiar only with old translations intended more to inspire than to transmit Thérèse's poetry as she wrote it.

Finally, in an effort to convey what Thérèse read as she read it, references to *The Rule and Constitutions* of the

Carmelite Order, *La Fables de la Fontaine,* and the French translation of the *Bible* in Chapter VIII, are based on 19th century French editions, presumably nearly identical to those actually used by Thérèse. Each was published between 1864 and 1875.

Abbreviations of Major Sources

CL	*Collected Letters of St. Thérèse of Lisieux*
DE	*Derniers Entretiens*
CG II	*Correspondance Générale. Tome II, 1890-1897*
GC I	*General Correspondance. Volume I, 1877-1890*
IC	*The Imitation of Christ*
LA	*St. Thérèse of Lisieux, her last conversations*
LC	Letters *to* Thérèse (cited in both French and English editions of her general correspondence)
LT	Letters *from* Thérèse
ME	Céline Martin's *A Memoir of My Sister St. Thérèse*
A	Manuscript A, autobiographical memories written by Thérèse for Pauline during the year 1895, first section of *Story of a Soul*
B	*Manuscript B*, written by Thérèse for Marie Martin September, 1896, second section of *Story of a Soul*
C	Manuscript C, autobiographical manuscript written for Mother Marie de Gonzague in June 1897, last section of *Story of a Soul*
TE	*St. Thérèse of Lisieux by those who knew her: testimonies from the process of beatification.*

Bibliography

Buber, Martin. *Two Types of Faith*. New York: Harper & Row, 1961.

Clarke, John. O.C.D. Trans. *St. Thérèse of Lisieux, Her Last Conversations*. Washington: Institute of Carmelite Studies, 1977. (Translation of *J'Entre Dans La Vie, Derniers Entretiens*. Paris: Desclée de Brouwer-Éditions du Cerf, 1973).

De Meester, Conrad. *Dynamique de la Confiance: Genèse et structure de la "voie d'enfance spirituelle" chez Ste. Thérèse de Lisieux. Paris:* Les Éditions du Cerf, 1969.

Foucauld, Charles de. *Meditations of a Hermit*. Charlotte Balfour, trans. New York: Orbis Books, 1930.

Gaucher, Guy. *Histoire d'Une Vie*. Paris: Les Éditions du Cerf, 1982.

The Jerusalem Bible. Gen Ed. Alexander Jones. N.Y.: Doubleday and Co., 1968.

John of the Cross. *The Collected Works of St. John of the Cross*. Kieran Kavanaugh, O.C.D. & Otilio Roderigues, O.C.D., Translators. Washington, D.C.: ICS Publications, 1979.

La Fontaine, Jean de. *Fables*. Paris: Garnier Frères, Libraires, 1864.

Lamm, Norman, *Faith and Doubt: Studies in Traditional Jewish Thought,* N.Y.: KTAV Publishing House Inc.,1971.

Laurentin, René. *Thérèse de Lisieux, Mythes et Realité*. Paris: Beauchesne, 1972.

Martin, Céline. *A Memoir of my Sister St. Thérèse.* New York: P.J. Kenedy & Sons, 1959.

Martin, Thérèse. (Sainte Thérèse de l'Enfant-Jesus et de la Sainte-Face). *Collected Letters of Saint Thérèse of Lisieux.* Ed. Abbé Combes. Trans. F.J. Sheed. New York: Sheed and Ward, 1949.

_____. *Correspondance Générale. Tome II 1890-1897.* Paris: Desclée de Brouwer-Éditions du Cerf, 1973.

_____. *Derniers Entretiens Avec Ses Soeurs Mere Agnes de Jesus, Soeur Genevieve, Soeur Marie du Sacre-Coeur et Temoignages Divers.* Paris: Desclée de Brouwer-Éditions du Cerf, 1971.

_____. *General Correspondence.* Vol I, 1877-1890. Trans. John Clarke, O.C.D. Washington: Institute of Carmelite Studies, 1982. (Translation of *Correspondance Générale Tome I 1877-1890.* Paris: Desclée de Brouwer-Éditions du Cerf, 1972.

_____. *La Bible avec Thérèse de Lisieux.* Desclée de Brouwer-Éditions du Cerf. Paris, 1979.

_____. *Manuscrits autobiographiques.* Francois de Sainte-Marie, O.C.D. trans. Lisieux: Carmel, 1957.

_____. *Poésies: un Cantique d'amour.* Desclée de Brouwer-Éditions du Cerf, 1979.

_____. *Story of a Soul.* John Clarke O.C.D. trans. Washington: Institute of Carmelite Studies, 1976. (Translation of *Histoire d'Une Âme,* Manuscrits autobiographiques. Paris: Desclée de Brouwer-Éditions du Cerf, 1972).

O'Connor, Patricia. *Thérèse Of Lisieux, A Biography.* Huntington, Indiana: Our Sunday Visitor, 1983.

O'Mahoney, Christopher, O.C.D. Ed. and trans. *St. Thérèse of Lisieux by those who knew her.* Huntington, Indiana: Our Sunday Visitor, 1975.

Piat, Stephane-Joseph, O.F.M. *Sainte Thérèse de Lisieux a la Decouverte de la Voie d'Enfance.* Paris: Éditions franciscaines, 1964.

Règle Primitive et Constitutions Dès Religieuses De l'Ordre de Notre-Dame Du Mont-Carmel Selon La Reformation De Sainte Thérèse Pour Les Monastères De Son Ordre En France. Poiters: Typographi De Henri Oudin, 1865.

Robert, Paul, *le Petit Robert, Dictionnaire alphabétique et analogique de la langue française.* Paris: Sociéte du Nouveau Littre, 1969.

Rohrback, Peter-Thomas, O.S.D., trans. *Photo Album of St. Thérèse of Lisieux,* New York: P. G. Kenedy and Sons, 1962. (Translations of *Visage de Thérèse de Lisieux,* Lisieux: Office Central).

Sacy, Le Maistre de. Translator. *La Sainte Bible.* Paris: Garnier Frères, 1875.

Six, Jean-Francois. *La Véritable Enfançe de Thérèse de Lisieux, Nervrose et Saintete.* Paris: Éditions du Seuil, 1973.

——————.Thérèse de Lisieux au Carmel. Paris: Éditions du Seuil, 1973.

Summarium. A summary of the process of beatification and canonization of Sister Thérèse of the Child Jesus. 1916, 1920. On file in the Archives of the Carmel of Lisieux.

Thomas à Kempis. *The Imitation of Christ.* Joseph N. Tylenda, S.J. trans. Michael Glazier, Inc.: Wilmington, Delaware, 1984.

Vénard, Théophane. Letter to Abbé Paziot (May 19, 1860), and letter to his family (January 20, 1861) in *Letters from the Saints* selected by a Benedictine of Stanbrook Abbey. New York: Hawthorn Books Inc., 1964.

Index